Boundless Prosperity

BOUNDLESS PROSPERITY
Prayer Book

Receive Abundant Financial Prosperity, Happiness,
Healing, Peace, Holiness,
and Much More

Reverend Ricardo Felix

Heavenly Miraculous Prayer Book

Copyright © 2019 Reverend Ricardo Felix.

All rights reserved. No part of this book may be used or reproduced by any means, graphic, electronic, or mechanical, including photocopying, recording, taping or by any information storage retrieval system without the written permission of the author except in the case of brief quotations embodied in critical articles and reviews.

WestBow Press books may be ordered through booksellers or by contacting:

WestBow Press
A Division of Thomas Nelson & Zondervan
1663 Liberty Drive
Bloomington, IN 47403
www.westbowpress.com
1 (866) 928-1240

Because of the dynamic nature of the Internet, any web addresses or links contained in this book may have changed since publication and may no longer be valid. The views expressed in this work are solely those of the author and do not necessarily reflect the views of the publisher, and the publisher hereby disclaims any responsibility for them.

Any people depicted in stock imagery provided by Getty Images are models, and such images are being used for illustrative purposes only.
Certain stock imagery © Getty Images.

NIV: THE HOLY BIBLE, NEW INTERNATIONAL VERSION®, NIV® Copyright © 1973, 1978, 1984, 2011 by Biblica, Inc.® Used by permission. All rights reserved worldwide.

ISBN: 978-1-9736-7734-5 (sc)
ISBN: 978-1-9736-7735-2 (hc)
ISBN: 978-1-9736-7733-8 (e)

Library of Congress Control Number: 2019916077

Print information available on the last page.

WestBow Press rev. date: 10/15/2019

ACKNOWLEDGMENTS

I Praise God the righteous Father who introduces me into a family of prayer warriors to become an eyewitness of the significance of prayer and be the direct beneficiary of it since my first month of infancy by miraculously healing me through the fervent prayer of my great grandmother Tissia Pierre. I am grateful also to the Holy Father for being there with me from all the process of writing this book, especially by laying his hand upon my head to heal me so I can complete this miraculous book joyfully without distress.

I praise also the Lord Jesus Christ who teaches me to pray and creates a path for me to witness the power of his name through prayer so I can write assertively this book for God's Glory. It is through his holy name that his Holy Father answers my countless of prayer requests to give me strength, wisdom, knowledge, inspiration and courage to complete this miraculously divine prayer book, *Boundless Prosperity*.

In addition, I am indebted to the Holy Ghost who supernaturally introduces me this awesome book and visually shows me the disciplinary strategies to successfully complete this book for the uttermost blessings of godly peoples everywhere.

Special thanks to the editorial staff of West Bow Press Janine David, Danielle Borst, Martin McHugh, Lucas Biery and everyone from this outstanding publishing company who guide me step by step wholeheartedly.

Special thanks also to my delightfully magnificent wife who engages herself in prayer and encourages me to keep the passion alive. Also to my sons Obed and Phinee who use qualified time in prayer for the success of this virtuous work.

Furthermore, to my prayerfully godly mother Solange Felix who remains steadfast in prayer from the beginning to the end for this work; finally, to many servants of God from many churches, specially Pastor Miche Chicoy, and Pastor Wesley Félix my younger brother who enthusiastically pray for this good work.

CONTENTS

Chapter 1	Biography	1
Chapter 2	Visible Presence of God on My family	8
Chapter 3	The Miraculous Events and Wonders of Writing This Book	11
Chapter 4	Origin of Prayer	14
Chapter 5	Heavenly Full Access of a Faithful Prayer	16
Chapter 6	Twelve Characteristics of Prayer as a Divine Significant Virtue	18
Chapter 7	Boundless Prosperity	25
Chapter 8	Financial Prosperity	27
Chapter 9	Happiness	30
Chapter 10	Prayer Sets	38
References		147

CHAPTER 1

Biography

I AM THE FOURTH GENERATION OF A DEVOTED Christian family. My great-grandmother Tissia Pierre was born at the end of the nineteenth century. She became a servant of God soon after her younger daughter married in 1930. She became also a devoted worker for the Lord Jesus Christ soon after receiving him at the First Baptist Church in Port-au-Prince, Haiti. The Lord bestowed on her many powerful spiritual gifts, including chastising demons and any type of evil spirit and healing people.

No demons or evil spirits could resist the authority of the Lord Jesus Christ through her. Through her, the Lord healed people with diseases doctors could not cure. She received the gift of prayer and was a mighty prayer warrior in her community.

The Lord gave her the gift of singing, through which she became the leading singer of her congregation. She received gracefully from God the gift of evangelism. She often walked many tens of miles to preach the gospel, and she helped build many churches.

Her relationship with the Lord was so excellent, I was told, that God never allowed her to get sick after her conversion, and she passed away without sickness. Two week before she passed away, the Holy Spirit acknowledged to her the time and manner of her death. She led a daily prayer at noon in the church every day except Sunday because that was worshipping service time.

After one of her noon prayers at First Baptist, when she was joyfully surrounded with all her loved ones and members of the congregation who came to pray and to witness this glorious event, Grandmother Tissia joyfully gave her soul to the Lord Jesus Christ, who took her to heaven in glory. She died at age seventy-one in perfect health.

She was the strength, the backbone of the family after her only daughter, Christiana Pierre, married and had ten children. Her daughter, my grandmother, was a devoted housewife and a faithful servant of the Lord who raised all her children to fear and love the living God. She was a magnificent, beautiful, and humble woman who gave her life to the Lord Jesus Christ in her teen years.

Her husband, Edouard Pierre, received the Lord Jesus about the same time as she did; by coincidence, they had the same last name. A few years after they got married, her husband spent his own money and built a church next to his house to serve the community because there was no church in the city where they lived.

That church grew in number rapidly, and Grandma Tissia was a prayer leader who brought excellent support to that Baptist congregation. My grandfather, as my uncles told me, was a strong, well-respected, God-fearing man who became the leader of that church. His nickname was Father Edouard because he loved to take care of people as he passionately led them into spiritual maturity. Today, that church still stands for the glory of God in the vicinity of Port-au-Prince. My grandfather and Grandma Tissia built other churches as well that still exist.

My mother, Solange Pierre, was the sixth of my grandparents' ten children. Born in 1943, she became Grandma Tissia's preferred daughter. Grandma Tissia made her mark in the community and in her family, and my mother carried much of her gift.

Grandma Tissia had a great impact on my life. She could recite all 150 psalms by heart, and she knew how to use them to chastise demons that were possessing people and to heal the sick. She was also a mighty reader of the Bible; she taught her grandchildren the psalms and how to pray and sing.

My mother knew many of the psalms because of Grandma Tissia, and she also became a prayer worrier and a lead singer with my grandmother's help; Grandma Tissia knew every song in the hymnal and taught them to my mother.

My mother played a leading role in the children's choir at the First Nazarene Church in Port-au-Prince, where she met my dad in 1951; they married when she was eighteen and he was twenty-two. They had four children, of whom I am the second and the second boy—three boys and one girl, who came last.

My dad was the foreman in charge of all construction for the Nazarene mission in Haiti; he worked for twenty years there and built churches in almost all the metropolitan areas in the country. Sometimes, he spent many weeks away from home; it was like a mission to him. He told me that he joyfully built churches in rural areas in Haiti. He worked with integrity in that mission until he came to the US in 1980. He served God faithfully and passed away in 2005 in Philadelphia of a heart attack, peace to his soul.

My dad waited until he was sixty-six to have a heart problem; however, heart disease has stalked me since I was a baby. One day, my mother saw that my behavior was unusual—I seemed almost dead—and she rushed me to the hospital. The doctor examined me and told my mom that my heartbeat was extremely slow; he could barely hear it. He told her that there was no chance I would live another day.

On the way home in tears, she met Grandma Tissia, who was on her way to see me and my mom. She took me from my mom and spent the whole afternoon and night in constant prayer. The next day, I became one of the healthiest babies in the world. God had perfectly healed my heart condition. She begged God all night in fervent prayer through psalms and songs and words of faith and won the favor of God.

That was one of the primary reasons the Holy Spirit guided me to write this book about all the blessings from prayer in my extended family and about how this true story had made a wonderful and positive impact on my life. The prayers in this book will be a great asset that will open heaven's doors for others so the mighty hands of God can pour overflowing blessings as a mighty stream. It will also allow everyone to receive favor and grace from God the Father and our Lord Jesus Christ.

My first clear recollection of my past was of being with my family in a Nazarene mission in a village almost one hour and a half from Port-au-Prince when I was two or three. It was surrounded by a vast forest. A road connected the village to Petionville, a city about 10 miles from the seminary.

The Nazarene mission took another expansion globally soon after the spiritual revival that had started in the US after World War II; it was made possible by Americans' massive prayers. By 1950, the mission had one or two churches in Haiti. Within twenty years, the Nazarene Church became one of the largest Protestant missions in Haiti.

This mission had a book publisher, a huge tabernacle for regular services, a seminary school equipped with dormitories, a church, and a basketball field, a giant cafeteria, many houses for the missionaries, a football field, an elementary school, a dispensary, and a workshop to build prefabricated materials for new churches.

A huge farm there raised pork, chickens, horses, and many acres of corn. As I recall, the place look like a little heaven with myrtle, plum, pine trees, and flowers that beautified the environment.

Our house was near the tabernacle, and we could see the beautiful mega church that received Nazarene members from all over the country. Worship services took place three times a week and every day during district assemblies. It was wonderful, and I would experience it again if I could. Seminary students came by our house for coffee and conversation. Many of them became friends for life.

The seminary was a place of worship and prayer where Nazarene church leaders and members of churches from many cities all over the country came together to celebrate the Lord Jesus Christ, to pray, to get instruction, and to continue expanding new churches through the propagation of the gospel in areas the Word of God had not reached.

I talked to those people and enjoyed their presence. I sensed a unity in prayer and sincere fraternity, and the Lord greatly blessed his work. That godly experience affected my prayer and worship life in a big way. I fully enjoyed the prayers, worship, and a variety of church activities; I witnessed the peace of God in me and all over that place. Christians at the Nazarene mission and I breathed what seemed to be heaven's air and became a family.

That experience allowed me to witness the deep peace of God, the joyful and loving manifestation of the Holy Spirit. Every time I visited that place during my teen and adult years, I felt that peace, love, and joy. When I dreamed of the mission, it was as if I were in heaven.

Music there was special; almost every instrument was played, including saxophones, trumpets, accordions, trombones, and guitars. I remember hearing seminary students practice the hymnal songs we sang at church.

My mother had an awesome voice, and she taught us the songs in the hymnal and the psalms when we prayed at night and in the morning. I was filled with the peaceful power of God and the Holy Spirit during those years, and my time living in the Nazarene seminary enriched my spiritual and prayer life forever.

Because my dad was often away building churches, my mom handled our discipline. Prayer time—morning, noon, and night—was a priority at home. At night and in the morning, we sang and recited many psalms and prayers that I still sing and recite. Over the years, the Holy Spirit gave me more psalms to pray for the world, for church leaders, my family, and people of my community for salvation, holiness, and revival.

My mother's concern for our education prompted our move to Delmas, a city with a full elementary and high school. We attended a Methodist and a Baptist church and at times the Church of God; my family had no problem doing that. I learned the Bible at those churches. When one hosted a visit from a special evangelist, we went. My family and an uncle helped establish a Nazarene church in Delmas that is still bringing people to salvation.

Through those experiences, I learned to work in many church positions—teaching in Sunday school, directing services, and evangelizing, and I saw the significance of prayer— impossible things becoming possible.

We moved to Queens, New York, in 1989, where my family helped a Nazarene minister we knew in Haiti start a ministry there, and we moved to Upper Darby Yeadon near Philadelphia in July 1990, where I helped churches.

In 1994, my younger brother and I received a call from God to attend seminary at Jameson School of Ministry in Pennsylvania, and we were ordained as ministers of the gospel. After a few years we became pastors of the Nazarene Church in Collingdale, Pennsylvania.

During that time, the Holy Spirit infused me with many gifts, including prayer; I felt such an urge to pray that I would wake up at three in the morning and pray for three hours. The psalm became fascinating to me. Every morning, I read many psalms, and I became zealous about attending church services, especially prayer services. I was inspired to ask more of God, and during night prayer services, the Holy Spirit would manifest in me like a wind in my head and ears.

The psalms have the glory of God. Among others, I recited Psalm 119 every morning. When I slept, the Holy Spirit showed me things that were going to happen to me that day. It was as if I relived that day. It lasted many weeks during 1994, a glorious year for me. Many times when I prayed in my room and praised the Lord, I saw a glowing light above my head. When I read the Bible, it also glowed. God's glorious light has been shining around me now for more than twenty years now.

In 1997, my brother and I passionately evangelized, and many people of different nationalities came to know the Lord Jesus Christ in Pennsylvania.

One day when I was praying in my room, the Holy Spirit instructed me to start a church in our house. I informed my family about it. We fixed the basement up very nicely, and my brother and I started offering children's Sunday school classes there. The Holy Spirit remind me that that was a great way to start because Jesus said, "Let the little children come to me, and do not hinder them, for the kingdom of God belongs to such as these" (Luke 18:16).

People in many homes we visited accepted the Lord Jesus Christ, and in a few months, we decided we needed a bigger location. Our church became a Nazarene church, and Wesley, my younger brother, is pastor there today. Through much prayer, God performed the mighty miracle of expanding and blessing the ministry he entrusted to us. The church grew greatly, and I was passionately doing the work God had called me to do.

When I was thirty-two and single, I prayed to the Lord Jesus for a spouse, and he revealed to me a beautiful girl who had received him as the Lord when she was nine. Juliette had come to the US when she was seventeen. We were about the same age when we married, and we had three boys—Frederick, Obed and Isaac Phinee Isaac Felix.

In 2001 in a vision, the Lord prompted me to move to Winter Park, Florida, to evangelize and encourage Christians who had not found congregations that spoke their languages. Many were senior citizens who were attending English-only worshipping churches if they were attending church at all due to the language barrier. I did the work of God in Altamonte Springs, East Orlando, Orlando, Kissimmee, and Clermont, and people were coming to know the Lord.

One day, the Holy Spirit asked me to start a church in Clermont, and I did so—in our one-bedroom apartment there. People who had been active in the Nazarene Church in Haiti found a place to worship in their native tongue.

The apartment soon became too small so we moved to a house, but that too soon became too small for our services. By the grace of God, a senior pastor at the First Baptist Church in Clermont learned of our need and offered us a big space in a building at his church. I became a co-pastor of the First Baptist Church in Clermont.

On morning while I was praying, the Holy Spirit guided me to go back to school and study anthropology. I completed a BA in anthropology in 2017 at the State University of Central Florida (UCF). God has sent me to another city to start a new congregation in Montverde, Florida.

I have witnessed through prayer how the Lord Jesus has blessed my parents financially. My family left Haiti not because of poverty but because of the political situation there. My father was always working. We had many houses and land that we rented out. I witnessed the power of tithing and offering from my parents and uncles and aunts. My parents' business has remained in Haiti until today. We never suffered a lack of financial resources. My mother's house in Pennsylvania is in a beautiful, middle-class neighborhood and is paid off. She became a pastor in a Nazarene church. God has blessed also all her children as they have been serving God.

My older brother had been a successful entrepreneur in Florida. My younger brother had been a pastor of the Nazarene church and entrepreneur. My sister, a physician, is the manager of a health department in Florida and is faithfully serving God. We all completed our academic education because our parents prayed for that ceaselessly to the Lord. Though I had ADD, which made it very hard for me to accomplish my academic studies, through faithful prayer, I graduated at last with distinction in anthropology. Obedience to the Word of God through continual prayer allowed the Lord Jesus Christ to guide us to boundless prosperity.

CHAPTER 2

Visible Presence of God on My family

Since I started doing ministry in Florida, the Holy Spirit provided me more spiritual gifts. I was able to clearly see evil spirits and demons in the invisible realm. In 2002, a Native American accepted the Lord Jesus Christ under my ministry, but a family spirit in charge of her saw that he had lost her and came to follow me. The Holy Spirit showed me that spirit, a departed ancestor of hers. I cast him away, and he never came back.

But in 2013, it took on another dimension. While I was walking into my room, the Holy Spirit gave me a vision of the Lord Jesus Christ wearing a crown and a royal-blue robe. I was saying a weekly prayer for governmental leaders, including kings and queens as the Bible commanded in Timothy. It usually took me more than two hours to say that prayer.

One day—October 13, 2013, a Sunday—I invited Obed, who was ten at the time, and Phinee, who was six, to pray with me for all the heads of government. I had the name of the heads of all countries in my folder ready, and the kids repeated them after me. The Lord Jesus opened the eyes of my Obed; he saw angels as we prayed. He said, "Daddy, I'm seeing a lot of angels!" I said, "Let me finish praying before you tell me about them" because I wanted to show God respect by finishing my prayer.

After we finished our prayer, I asked Obed, "What did you see?"

He said he had seen the Lord Jesus in front of me wearing a shining golden cloth. He said he had not been able to see his face because it was shining like the sun, but he had seen his crown. Its sides were blue, and it had a pink diamond in the middle. He said the Lord Jesus had been looking at me. He told me that he had felt a strong peace. He said there were many angels in the house, one of whom was standing by the Lord Jesus Christ with a fiery golden spear.

He said a lot of black angels were guarding our back porch with golden arrows. The house was full of black, white, and golden angels, one of whom was a beautiful female he had fallen in love with. He told me that the Lord Jesus had told him his name was Yahweh. Obed said that one of the angels had touched Phinee with his sword and that a demon had come out of him and left. Obed told me I was wearing a silver crown and golden armor.

He said also that there were many angels flying above the house and patrolling our yard. Obed said that he had seen the angels start to leave when I finished my prayer.

How could my son have explained to me in detail the colors of their dress, skin, hair, sandals, their attitude of that celestial presence, their position in the house and outside and how he had felt so peaceful while I was praying? I believed it was the truth.

For about a year, the Lord and his holy angels continued to manifest himself visibly through Obed's eyes every time he and I and Phinee prayed. Many times, the Lord Jesus Christ came with his Holy Father.

It would take another book to explain the details Obed saw. The three persons of God have manifested visibly to me also but not as they had manifested to Obed. He could see them for many hours or more as I prayed that year. He has seen the whole face of the Lord Jesus Christ. He also saw God the Father many times but not his face because it shined like the sun as had Jesus's face the first time Obed saw it. Phinee also saw God many times in 2013 and 2014.

After 2014, the Holy Spirit decided not to visibly manifest through Obed and Phinee's eyes, and they became discouraged about praying my prayer for the world's leaders. I did not force them; I continued to pray by myself. I understood prayer for more than two hours for the world was not an easy sacrifice. However, sometimes when they felt they wanted to pray, they joined me.

During my personal time of prayer and praising God, he manifested visibly to me three times. Many times, the Holy Spirit shined like the sun above my head while I was praising him. Jesus Christ appeared visibly to me more than five times in my room. One night in April 2017, I was singing "Worthy is the lamb of God" when I saw the Lord Jesus Christ on his golden throne for perhaps ten seconds. I continued to pray and sing a song the Holy Spirit inspired me to sing from the book of Revelation, something my family and I sang frequently. This is part of it.

Worthy is the Lamb of God (three times).
Bless the Lord Jesus Christ's holy name (twice).
To receive honor, glory, riches, and blessing.
To receive knowledge, wisdom, and strength (twice).

I wrote these testimonies so you and I could see prayer as our ultimate blessing to attract the glory of God and magnify him in daily life. Faithful prayer will secure your boundless prosperity and the cause the blessed and prosperous abundance of God to shine out like dawn from us.

Through prayer, the Holy Spirit gives us the grace and favor to witness God's wonders. God has also spoken out lout to Obed and Phinee during moments of prayer and praise. Almost all my blessings and miracles came when I was in prayer.

CHAPTER 3

The Miraculous Events and Wonders of Writing This Book

About fifteen years ago, I had a desire to know more about how to pray more effectively because it has been a gift the Holy Spirit gave me in 1993. As I spent tremendous time in prayer, I recognized my extreme limitations; unwise prayers could keep me from producing more godly fruit.

I read many books about prayer, and my understanding of prayer changed radically. I learned that prayer was not for my satisfactions only; it was also a way to please the Lord and to accomplish God's purpose for my life. Prayer had to be in accord with the Word of God. God was preparing me for many decades to write this book.

In 2017, I attended a thanksgiving ceremony at a Nazarene church in Philadelphia. I was inspired to ask the church leaders to pray for me for this book. Four ministers and two faithful servants of God laid their hand on me and prayed for this endeavor, but once I was back in Florida, though I continued engaging in ministry, I felt no strength or motivation to write even a paragraph.

But one night in May 2018, while I was praying before going to sleep, the Holy Spirit asked me to open my hands. I did, though I did not understand the request because the Holy Spirit always spoke to me through sign. I asked the Lord to manifest the power of his seven spirits in my life, and while I was praying, I saw a book coming from above and getting in to my right hand; God showed me that he favorably answered what I had requested in that prayer also.

The next night, I opened my hand to praise the Lord and saw information on how to start this book on my left hand. The next day, I had the motivation, strength, and inspiration to start writing. I realized I was supposed to write a prayer book, and I got to work on that divine project, which became my most important mission.

How to Use This Book of Prayer

I started writing using the Bible as the Lord had inspired me to do so I could write the book in perfect accord with the Word of God. God inspired me to write a practical book of prayer with a comprehensive 192 sets of prayers consisting of twenty-four sets of daily prayer in eight days. It was to be a lifetime book of practical prayers according to the inspiration the Holy Spirit. I knew I would use this book to help me succeed and prosper financially as well as spiritually.

The eight days symbolize the resurrection day of the Lord Jesus Christ, the new day or the day of the Lord. The twenty-four daily sets represented the twenty-four elders in Revelation. Two and four equal six, the number of man that meant it was a book to bring humanity to serve God in boundless prosperity.

The twenty-four sets of daily prayers are divided—twelve sets are to be used in the morning and twelve before we go to sleep. From the one hundred ninety two sets of prayers, the numbers one, nine, and two added equal twelve, the number for God's government, so this book was also meant to pray for governmental leaders in the world also. From the number twelve, One and two added equal three, which represents the Trinity; this is a divine book of prayer that will bring humanity closer to God.

Personal Healing Miracle while Typing This Prayer Book

Genesis through Revelation inspired the prayers in this book. While I was typing one day, I saw the hand of God on my head. I have suffered from ADD from birth because of a heart defect that my grandmother prayed for healing for as I mentioned earlier. Nonetheless, my heart condition had a side effect: it made me very slow to do any work. That was one reason it took me eight years to obtain a BA in anthropology. My impairment affects my speed when I type, and it causes stress and some pain on my brain. I have consulted many neurologists, psychologists, and psychiatrists and prayed all my life for a healing, but it has stayed the same. As a result, I do everything slowly and with some distress.

But after I saw God's hand on my head while I was typing prayers for this book, He healed me instantly. I heard a noise in my brain; it was as if a heavy weight came off my head. I was then able to speed up my typing very remarkably with no pain or distress.

As I typed the prayers, I used them as personal prayers. God downloaded them into my mind and healed me mightily. After that, typing became fun rather than a burden. I thank God for delivering me from my affliction. Even when I was far from finishing this book, God honored the prayers of this book to heal me. Since that time, I became fully certain that this book would prompt many miracles of healing and prosperity in people's lives.

CHAPTER 4
Origin of Prayer

BECAUSE PRAYER HAS ALWAYS BEEN A fundamental element in the lives of the people of God, it makes sense to ask what prayer is and what its origin is. Prayer is basically a solemn request for help from the almighty God, a way to show gratitude to him, and a way to praise him for his goodness.

The Bible tells us that the Lord Jesus Christ was a sovereign sacrificator in the manner of Melchizedek, king of Salem, who has no beginning, as the book of Hebrews reveals. The role of a sacrificator is to make atonement for the people and to intercede on their behalf.

Hebrews clearly reveals that the Lord Jesus Christ's existence is before the beginning of the world as an eternal sovereign sacrificator. He has been always that way before his Holy Father, before time began, to make intercession for us. Even before we were created, our Lord was making requests for all of us to his Father to assist us mostly in regard to salvation. From this revelation, I can declare that prayer originated in the Godhead for all eternity as the Lord Jesus Christ has always been an eternal sacrificator without father or mother.

I truly believe, as prayer is always a practical virtue within God himself from all eternity past, it is also a necessity within him to deal perfectly toward all his creation forever. We witness this fact through the life of the Lord Jesus Christ during his time of ministry on earth about two thousand years ago.

As children of God on Earth who carry God's image and call to follow the Lord Jesus Christ footsteps, it is mandatory and a tremendous necessity for all of us to fervently and consistently pray if we want to live a successfully perfect life in this World.

CHAPTER 5
Heavenly Full Access of a Faithful Prayer

AT WORK, TEAM LEADERS INSTRUCT OTHERS how to accomplish tasks, and those doing the work ask for what they need to accomplish their tasks, including equipment and training.

It's the same with prayer. God, our team leader, gives us instruction on how to serve him, and we ask him for what we need to make us successful and productive spiritually, financially, and socially. When we stay within the perimeter of his Word and talk to him and obey him, our prayers will give us access to his throne and receive favorable answers from him.

The prayers of God's obedient children give them everything they ask from the Lord. God will help all people live obedient lives when they come to him with contrite hearts in prayer. The main purpose of this book's prayers is to allow the Holy Spirit to empower, inspire, heal, and guide all to the right path so they can become spiritually mature and devout servants of God in holy living through God's prosperous blessings.

Through prayer, we children of God can put a lot of angels to work on our behalf; that is what he provided his faithful servants in the Bible. When Daniel and the faithful Israelites in captivity in Babylon prayed, God sent the Archangel Michael with an army of warrior angels to fight against the king of Prussia in the invisible realm to deliver his people. Faithful prayers give us direct access to heaven and enable God to come to our rescue, satisfy our needs, and help us receive every blessing he wants us to have. Children of God can experience boundless success in any discipline and domain through faithful prayer.

Many people do not see their prayers answered because they do not understand the purpose of prayer—to develop a good, holy, and faithful relationship with God. When that is understood, we will have full access to God and receive financial prosperity and every other blessings he promised people in the Bible.

When prayer is in accordance with the Word, when his children are in harmony with the guidance of the Holy Spirit and respect the sovereignty of the will of God, he will grant what they ask. The prayers in this book are in perfect accord with the Word of God and his will. It also empowers the church to walk according to the Holy Spirit and brings us victory in every domain.

CHAPTER 6

Twelve Characteristics of Prayer as a Divine Significant Virtue

Its Origin

AS I MENTIONED, PRAYER HAS ALWAYS BEEN AN active factor of the Godhead; the Bible revealed that the Word of God was a person—the King of righteousness and sovereign sacrificator who had no beginning and has no end and intercedes for others.

Through this virtue, the wisdom of God had been established for creation to have its purpose and to satisfy the desires of all the persons in the Godhead. As a result, people in the church became the children of God the Father, the bride of the Lord Jesus Christ, and the temple of the Holy Spirit.

The Word of God reveals to us that the Holy Spirit also prayed to God the Father on our behalf so we could have the power to overcome sins by fulfilling the good work and instructions our Lord provided us.

Coherent Relationship between Prayer and Faith

When you and I pray, we exercise the power of faith as long we believe that God truly answers us. If there is faith in our prayers, they please God and he acts on our behalf. Individuals who successfully prayed always relied on faith. As I explained before, faith came from the Word of God. When there was no dust of the earth and in the universe, God believed it was possible to bring forth creation, and creation came to be; it started with faith. Faith has always been a tangible part of God because he resided in his Word. God had always possessed a bold and unfailing assurance to hope for everything he wanted to do that has been the definition of faith.

However, God conveyed this blessing to all of us. That is why the Bible said, "If my people humbled themselves and seek my face and repented of their wicked ways I will hear to deliver them of every of their problems." When we were in accord with the Word of God and remained in constant prayer every day to pray as the Word of God required, anything we asked became possible because the Word of God always possessed faith.

Prayer—An Outstanding Asset to Help Us Apply the Word of God

Prayers in agreement with the Word of God that are specific on the virtue of God will empower his children to be fully spiritually mature.

The Lord Jesus Christ said that if we asked his Father good things, he would provide them to us because God the Father always rejoiced to bless his holy people. When you and I cried sincerely to God our Father to empower us to obey him better or to give us victory over a spiritual weaknesses, that would get his attention and please him because he would see we took great concern to please him and to live holy, which has always been God's priority for our lives.

However, God has already made preparation for all of us in his beloved Son Jesus Christ; we need to know the process as the book of James explains it. All wise and godly church leaders must do what is necessary to implement the resources to successfully help immature believers in peril to spiritually overcome any sin in their lives. Qualified members in the congregation must be ready to counsel and pray with immature believers to help them obey the Word of God. That was why James 5:16 declared, "The prayer of a righteous person is powerful and effective." So prayer can bring down the power and favor of God on the lives of believers for perfect obedience to the Word of God by the faithful prayers of the righteous individual.

Prayer's Transversal Power

The transversality of prayer is limitless; it can reach everything and can better everything in life and even reach things not yet come. That is why prayer is so significant to God and must be to us. Jesus Christ while on earth prayed for you and me to allow his Holy Father to preserve us from the wickedness of this world. Prayer will better the politic of this world—our society, our justice system, our personal health, the health system in this world, and our spiritual life. Prayer will help ensure God's blessing for us. Prayer will bring God's attention to us.

Remember the prayer of Moses through which he stopped the wrath of God on the disobedient Israelites. Prayer causes the people of God to return to their homeland from captivity in Babylon. Remember the prayer of Daniel. Prayer caused God to financially bless Jabez abundantly. It is through the prayer of the Lord Jesus Christ that the apostle Peter became faithfully victorious when the Lord said, "Simon, Simon, Satan has asked to sift you like wheat. But I have prayed for you, Simon that your faith will not fail."

Prayer Motivates Us to Manifest God's Creative Power

Prayer exalts the Word of God and empowers it to manifest his creative power. When the people of God were in captivity in Egypt, as long as they kept on complaining to God, they remained in slavery, but when they started calling to God, he intervened to demonstrate his miraculous power—ten plagues and one of the greatest creative miraculous and powerful works of God—parting the Red Sea.

Prayer Affects a Mutually Trilateral Divine Relationship

Prayer nourishes a mutually trilateral relationship in the Godhead that serves to facilitate God's plan of God to satisfy all in the Godhead. It is also to put in motion the will of God about everything he wants to create in a reciprocal way to satisfy the Trinity. Prayer engenders an agreement in the divine counsel who brings creation to order because everything God does is based on a mutual divine relationship in its Godhead; those in the Godhead pray to each other.

Prayer Prompts Humility

Prayer manifests and magnifies humility and gives the possibility to both parties to practice humility, first from God, who is receiving the request, and then the one praying. When descent vulnerable individual brings their request to arrogant leaders, they usually bring down and reject the demand requested. However, God is not like that; he takes seriously our requests specially those of his holy children. The Bible says that when the just cry, Yahweh pays attention and satisfies their demand. When we as children of God pray, he listens and grants our requests; that is pure humility from the almighty God.

It is also an act of humility to make personal requests for our needs and make requests on behalf of someone else because we have to lower ourselves to go before God. Humbleness is a significant virtue of God that makes relationships productive and satisfactorily friendly because humility will naturally make the children of God accept the patience of God. King David showed long patience in prayer to wait to be enthroned as king of Israel. Our waiting on God in prayer is a pleasing act of humility in his eyes.

Prayer is one of the characteristics of God that shows humility. Prayer is the quintessence of humbleness, which opens the door of our heart for patience. Humble people are patient people.

Prayer Allows Us to Receive God's Blessings

Rightful, upright, and godly prayers help believers live successful, holy, and sanctified lives with immense fear of the Lord, which is the beginning of wisdom. Prayers empower the children of God to be independent of the false joy and happiness the world provides, which can deceive them and prevent them from receiving God's perfect and immeasurable joy, happiness, and contentment.

Virtuous prayer gives believers zeal to worship God and serve him. Constant and godly prayers by people of God for the salvation of the world will bring global revival and an outpouring of the Holy Spirit in the world that will convince billions to repent and receive the Lord Jesus Christ as their personal Savior and Lord.

Prayers according to the Word will empower his holy people to faithfully use the principle of prosperity in terms of sowing and reaping so they can live prosperously.

Prayers provide the servants of God with his favor and grace to have perfect physical health, spiritual healing, and stability. A lifetime commitment to prayer will ensure in the lives of every believer a holy personal fulfilment and satisfaction with perfection from the presence of God in their souls. Faithful prayer will also bring God's strength and power to help them walk perfectly faithful with excellence before God in fervent love for the Lord and all people. With bold and upright prayer to do God's works, we will be productive with the gifts God entrusts to us.

These are just some examples of what godly prayers will do in our lives. Prayer can touch everything in the present and future. Prayer is the transversal tool of God that manifests his infinite power and the love he freely gives us.

Prayer Magnifies Thanksgiving and Petition

When we pray and ask God for something, we should remember the next time we pray for that same thing to thank the Lord for that blessing, which is on its way though we have not received any response from the Lord. This is significant to God because he takes pleasure from this practice; it is bold act of faith and a demonstration of gratitude; it proves that we believe God will give us what we request from him. Most pray in thanksgiving after they receive things from God, but in the Bible, many times, our Lord thanked his Father for things that had not happened yet. When the Lord was going to resurrect Lazarus, he thanked his Father for answering him even before the miracle occurred. He did that with the few fishes and the bread that were multiplied to feed a multitude.

Giving God thanks before the answers to our prayers materialize enhances our faith and expectation, a powerful key to unlock the door of heaven so we can obtain what we ask God for.

Taking our petition or concern to God will allow us to live peacefully (Philippians 4:6–7) and help us overcome our problems because God can make the impossible possible. Certain things are beyond our capacity but not beyond God's.

Prayer Glorifies God

A prayerful life will allow God to manifest his glorious power to show humanity new wonders above their limitations. Moses, during an intense prayer with God, asked him to manifest himself before the people, and God did so as a pillar of smoke by day and a pillar of fire at night. The prayers of holy servants of God are significant to him.

You and I as God's children can suffer terrible spiritual problems, but if we lower ourselves to request prayer and counseling from holy servants of God, the Bible says he will heal us. Prayer allows the people of God to overcome sin when it is used right.

God's virtues will manifest in the lives of his servants if their prayers are well practiced. The Bible says we should pray always. Jesus Christ accomplished his Father's will by making prayer the pillar of his ministry on earth. One of his main jobs right now in his Father's temple is to pray on our behalf so we can possess the virtues of God to live holy lives.

Prayer Affects Spiritual Revival

Prayer can spiritually revive churches in every sector. As prayer is transversally limitless and powerful, when people use it for spiritual revival, the graceful power of God is mightily witnessed to bring people to repentance and salvation.

Consider the impact of Jonah's prayers during his three days in the big fish—the conversion of Nineveh. Consider the result of Pentecost—the Holy Spirit fell on the disciples and in one day, three thousand came to know Jesus Christ.

At the end of World War II, Christians in the US felt an urge to pray for revival as the war had distressed so many families the world over. God listened to his people and poured out the power of the Holy Spirit in the world by bringing a global spiritual revival. Evangelist Billy Graham became the forefront of this mighty event, and many other evangelists traveled the US and abroad to open new congregations, and US missionaries spread the gospel overseas, all as a result of prayer.

Prayer Limits the Power of Evil

Evil has been at work since the Garden of Eden. Many times, God chose to deliver his people from the kingdom of darkness and raised mighty men of prayer to counterattack the devil. Moses delivered his people from slavery under the false gods in Egypt. King David led the people in godliness and protected the Israelites from idol-worshipping nations. Daniel and the exiled people in Babylon brought down the graceful power of God to fight the evil powers from the heaven by the Almighty's holy angelic armies presided by Archangel Michael to allow God to bring the people of Israel back to their homeland so they could worship him in the temple in Jerusalem.

His beloved Son Jesus Christ, the apostles, and the disciples up until the third century were disciplined in prayer and brought people from wickedness to salvation. Through such mighty men of prayer, God defeated the realm of darkness and saved his people from bondage.

In this millennium, God will raise men and women of prayer like you and me to carry on this honorable task because the battle is not over. We can pray together or alone in our houses the prayers in this book and others provided by our church leaders for the same purpose—to defeat the work of the kingdom of darkness everywhere and limit the destructive power of evil.

All our prayers will empower humanity to be delivered from the lies and the deceitfulness of the destroyer of our souls who puts our world in spiritual peril.

CHAPTER 7
Boundless Prosperity

THE GREATEST BLESSING GOD GIVES US IS THE Bible, his Holy Word. He gave us his only begotten Son so we could have eternal life—God himself, whose attributes are limitless. God reveals them through his creation—hundreds of billions of stars and many billions of galaxies give us an idea how powerful he is.

His holiness is revealed through his character, the essence of his person demonstrated throughout the Bible. His holiness makes him a living God,

apart from whom is death. Everything good comes from him, and he sustains and prospers his creation.

To obtain God's limitless riches, humanity needs to be delivered from sin, which opposes everything God stands for. Sin is death, the source of all the trouble in the universe. Sin is disobedience to the Word of God. Sin is also a crime to the almighty God personally. Sin caused Adam and Eve to reject God's boundless prosperity and eternal life.

Jesus Christ stated in John 17:3, "Now this is eternal life: that they know you, the only true God, and Jesus Christ, whom you have sent." God offers us all eternal life. All must have this boundless prosperity to live eternally and manifest God's character and glory. That was why Jesus Christ affirmed, "I am the resurrection and the life. The one who believes in me will live, even though they die" (John 11:25). Those who have accepted Jesus Christ will live holy lives in boundless prosperity; their lives cannot fail when they obey him sincerely.

If everybody in this world had this life, there would be no hunger, violence, or poverty and everyone would live peacefully and in full security. Abuse and war would end, and no one would be exploited. Boundless prosperity is a rich and godly way of living that causes the world to live in harmony. God's way of living is true living.

Boundless prosperity is the essence of God manifesting in our lives and souls and produces joy, peace, love, faith, hope, and security in our hearts. Through God, we can fulfill our true purpose in life. Prayers are tremendous assets that empower the people of God to unfailingly witness the boundless prosperity of God personally in their lives.

CHAPTER 8
Financial Prosperity

"Bring the whole tithe into the storehouse, that there may be food in my house. Test me in this," says the Lord Almighty, "and see if I will not throw open the floodgates of heaven and pour out so much blessing that there will not be room enough to store it. I will prevent pests from devouring your crops, and the vines in your fields will not drop their fruit before it is ripe," says the Lord Almighty. "Then all the nations will call you blessed, for yours will be a delightful land," says the Lord Almighty. (Malachi 3:10–12)

THE GOD OF ABRAHAM and Jacob said that. The Almighty instructs his people that he will financially bless his people when they tithe and make offerings as the above verses state.

Christians who trust the Lord to faithfully apply this financial principle and live obediently before God will witness the power of God through their financial lives and businesses. Our sovereign God will favor those who respect his instructions and practice them. He will cause their fields to produce mighty harvests and prosper their businesses.

People of the living God, Yahweh Jireh cannot lie; the Bible says, "What his mouth says, his hand will accomplish." If we make a bold commitment to obey the Word of God concerning tithing and offering and live holy and humble lives, we will personally witness financial wealth—God's guarantee to us.

Financial riches were given to humanity only to magnify the boundless riches of God and demonstrate his love. He makes the sun rise on the good and the wicked because of his love. So we all have to financially support our church communities and God's work everywhere to be blessed mightily by the Lord.

Financial Prosperity

> Remember this: Whoever sows sparingly will also reap sparingly, and whoever sows generously will also reap generously. Each of you should give what you have decided in your heart to give, not reluctantly or under compulsion, for God loves a cheerful giver. And God is able to bless you abundantly, so that in all things at all times, having all that you need, you will abound in every good work. (2 Corinthians 9:6–8)

This passage reconfirms the principle of giving to support the work of God his servants are performing. The Lord told us this in Luke 6:38. Isaiah 58 explains all the benefits of giving to the poor and financially supporting the vulnerable. Elsewhere in the Bible, God commanded us to financially support fatherless children and widows who are struggling.

Tithing is the minimum God commands us to give. The

Word of God clearly enumerates that the more we give, the more blessing we will receive. The apostle Paul exemplified giving as sowing seeds that we will later reap. He asked the Christians in Corinth for additional offerings, love offerings, in addition to tithes to support the ministers of God. The apostle Paul ensured those in the church of Corinth that this extra giving was to support him while tithes supported the church. The apostle ensured the believers in Corinth that such additional giving would result in an overflow of financial and other blessings—the more they sowed, the more they would reap. Jesus Christ explained to his disciples and followers the same principle.

The Word of God shows us the effects of giving, for instance, the multiplication of the few loaves and fish that fed the multitudes and left twelve baskets full of bread and fish. Those who give will receive more than tenfold or hundredfold in return.

In another example of giving, God the Father gave his Son and received countless souls in return; today, more than a billion Christians are his children. I have witnessed this principle of giving in my life and in the lives of my mom and dad, two brothers, and my sister.

The Lord Jesus Christ proclaimed to us, "Give, and it will be given to you. A good measure, pressed down, shaken together and running over, will be poured into your lap" (Luke 6:38).

CHAPTER 9

Happiness

> You have made known to me the paths of life; you will fill me with joy in your presence. (Acts 2:28)

IN THE PRESENCE OF GOD, JOY IS A MIGHTY river. Happiness is an infinite gift from God and one of his limitless characteristics as is prosperity. God's loving presence among his holy people brings happiness to all his children along with his love, peace, holiness, omniscience, self-sufficiency, and his other characteristics.

God is the quintessence of happiness and joyfulness. He does not depend on anyone or anything outside himself for his pure happiness. King David witnessed this glorious and awesome characteristic when he testified that his soul encountered a fully joyful fulfilment in the presence of God.

The Word of God commands believers to rejoice in the Lord Jesus Christ through song, praise, exaltation, and thanksgiving and though prayers and petition with thanksgiving to God so we can live joyfully and in peace. The Almighty is the source of his people's happiness.

Those who rely on drugs, alcohol, entertainment, pleasures from social media, sports, and financial gain without the presence of God go crazy looking for more of the same harmful things that will never satisfy them; rather, they will be pushed toward violence, greed, stealing, hurting each other, and sin in general.

We Christians who live faithfully in God even though we might have little money at times live fully satisfied because the joy and happiness of the Lord is perfect in our hearts all the time. That empowers us to love God, ourselves, and everyone else. We receive the Lord's joy, which is freely offered to us by the blood of the Lord Jesus Christ.

Faithful prayer to the living God is an outstanding virtue our God provides all of us. He can immensely increase his peaceful and joyful presence in our soul to nullify our distress and sorrow. Faithful prayers are powerful tools that embolden our joy and happiness by the holy presence of the Lord Jesus Christ in us when challenges of life threaten our souls. That is a tremendous blessing from God.

The Lord Jesus Christ boldly affirmed to his disciples, "Until now you have not asked for anything in my name. Ask and you will receive, and your joy will be complete" (John 16:24). That is why the prayers in this book are directed to God the Father and are expressed through the mighty name of the Lord Jesus Christ. They will enable us to be fully and satisfactorily enjoyable as we say these faithful prayers.

INTRODUCTION TO PRAYER SETS

Efficient and Beneficial Ways for Your Blessed Anointing

As I mentioned, the most powerful way to activate our faith after we pray to God for something is to thank God as if he has already answered our prayer.

If you are considering buying a house, for instance, you can describe to God in prayer exactly how you want to receive this blessing. The next time you pray about the matter, thank God for providing it, and he will surely do so. Sometimes, patience is needed to be applied, but the answer will surely come to pass.

However, repetitive prayer is a way of receiving God's anointing to do extraordinary things because every time we pray for the same thing, our souls will receive additional anointing. This is especially the case when we ask God for guidance, strength, patience, wisdom, joy, and power for success and to overcome life's obstacles. The Lord demonstrated this when he prayed in the Garden of Gethsemane. Mark 14, Luke 22, Matthew 26, and John 17 clearly affirm this practice of the Lord Jesus Christ.

Anointing is like software that can be downloaded into the soul but to have it in overflowing measure, it makes easier to accomplish successfully many tasks that result in a harvest of financial and spiritual blessings.

A powerful way to immensely increase anointing is through prayer. I wrote *Boundless Prosperity* to show that repetitive prayer ensures children of God continuous resupply of God's anointing in greater measure. It is a lifetime book for any child of God to use. It contains an overflowing of prayer requests to take to the Lord that will enrich readers with a great quantity of diversified divine anointing that will overflow in their souls so they can enjoy boundless prosperity from the Almighty, who dwells in their souls.

God, the creator of all human beings, endows anointing on us for his glory. He knows all people before they are even born. In his goodness, he makes substantial provisions for them to fulfill their destinies in life through his anointing. God can administer additional anointing to his children to do some specific tasks for his glory, as was the case with King David, whom the prophet Samuel anointed king.

The great news for all of us today is that everyone in Christ Jesus can claim an immense quantity and variety of anointing through a personal relationship with God through prayer. Through prayer, we can be empowered to practice perfectly with boldness and passion the principles required to receive the Almighty's financial and spiritual harvest, to live holy lives, to do unimaginable things—all for the glory of God.

Peoples who have less anointing in some area of their lives can receive the passion they need to fulfill the tasks given to them through prayer and gain financial prosperity, holiness, creativity, and success in many areas in their lives, but that requires continuous and repetitive prayer. Remember that the Lord Jesus used prayer to overcome his extremely sorrowful challenges to endure perfectly the cross.

Repetitive prayer will help everyone achieve victory and receive an overflowing anointing of love, humility, truth, patience, kindness, godliness, godly sexual morality, and obedience to God's Word and instructions.

Repetitive prayer will enable God to release anointing for academic and financial success and wisdom in any area of life to overcome challenges. Give your difficulties to God in prayer, and you will receive the anointing of the Almighty.

I know many giant holy servants of the living God who are mighty men and women of prayer and achieve unthinkable things for God almighty such as Queen Esther, the mother of the prophet Samuel, the mother of president George Washington, my great-grandmother Tissia Pierre, Jane Crouch from TBN and her husband, the eminent Paul Crouch, the Reverend Dr. T. D. Jake, Pastor Joel Osteen, the Pastor Evangelist Jimmy Swaggart, the Prophet T. B Joshua in Algeria, the Prophet Daniel in the Bible, our dearly unchallengeable and unmatchable the Lord Jesus Christ, the apostles Peter, John, and Paul, and two rising giants in the Haitian Christian community—Reverend Dr. Andre Muscadin from Shalom Ministry and Pastor Gregory Toussaint from Shekinah Glory Ministry, and finally, the unforgettable evangelist Billy Graham. All of them made their marks on their communities or throughout the world for God because of their devotion to passionately and faithfully use prayer as the pillar in their lives as a prioritized tool for the glory of God.

Today, everyone who knows the living God answers prayer should make their marks on their families, communities, and the world by personally witnessing to the power of God's anointing through their prayers from this book.

It is a privilege and honor that the holy Father miraculously provided me this book through the leadership of the Holy Spirit to empower his children to better and more productively honor him and his beloved Son Jesus Christ, his Holy Word, so everyone could joyfully experience more of his boundless prosperity and anointing he gladly makes available to prosperously bless his children through their prayers. God said he takes pleasure in the prosperity of all his saints.

The biblical passages below will encourage you, strengthen your faith in prayer, and generate a passionate and devout desire to pray in you.

> I urge, then, first of all, that petitions, prayers, intercession and thanksgiving be made for all people, for kings and all those in authority, that we may live peaceful and quiet lives in all godliness and holiness. (1 Timothy 2:1–2)
>
> Pray continually. (1 Thessalonians 5:17)
>
> Devote yourselves to prayer, being watchful and thankful. (Colossians 4:2)

Do not be anxious about anything, but in every situation, by prayer and petition, with thanksgiving, present your requests to God. (Philippians 4:6)

Then Jesus told his disciples a parable to show them that they should always pray and not give up. (Luke 18:1)

One of those days Jesus went out to a mountainside to pray, and spent the night praying to God. (Luke 6:12)

The Lord is near to all who call on him, to all who call on him in truth. (Psalm 145:18)

And I will do whatever you ask in my name, so that the Father may be glorified in the Son. You may ask me for anything in my name, and I will do it. (John 14:13-14)

He will respond to the prayer of the destitute; he will not despise their plea. (Psalm 102:17)

Watch and pray, so that you will not fall into temptation. The spirit is willing, but the flesh is weak. (Matthew 26:41)

Therefore, I tell you, whatever you ask for in prayer, believe that you have received it, and it will be yours. (Mark 11:24)

Ensure a Faithful Godly Relationship

If you want to acquire all the blessing God wants to give his children who are in his beloved son Jesus Christ, first receive the Lord Jesus Christ in your life. John 3:16 reads, "For God so loved the world that he gave his one and only Son, that whoever believes in him shall not perish but have eternal life." John 1:12 reads, "Yet to all who did receive him, to those who believed in his name, he gave the right to become children of God."

If you do not yet have the Lord Jesus Christ in your heart to wipe away your sins, say this simple prayer and God will take care of your sins. Then you will formally be a child of God and fully benefit from the prayers in this book as you will do your best to live in obedience to God's holy Word. Say in your heart and out loud this prayer.

Lord Jesus Christ,
I believe you were crucified on the cross and shed your blood for my sins.
I believe you were also resurrected from death for my eternal life.
I repent of all my sins against God, your Holy Father.
I accept you as my Lord and Savior and will obey you and please you all my life.
Come now into my heart to dwell and to save my soul.

If you are a Christian who is not totally faithful to God, you can recommit your life to God to fully benefit from the faithful prayers in this book by repeating this short prayer.

Holy Father, I recommit my life to fully pleasing you by obeying the Lord Jesus Christ as my master and Lord. In the name of the Lord Jesus Christ I pray.

Those who just accepted the Lord Jesus Christ as their Savior and Lord or recommitted their lives to God should read the Bible every day to practice what the Word of God says. The New King James Version (NKJV) and the New International Version (NIV) are the best I know. Read the New Testament by starting with Matthew, the first book. Pray to God to help you find a good church if you do not have one. God will not let any of his faithful children be condemned to hell forever because the Lord Jesus took on hell by being crucified on the cross for those who receive him in their lives as Lord and Savior.

When prayer is in accord with the Word of God and God's children are in perfect harmony with the guidance of the Holy Spirit and respect the sovereignty of the will of God, he will grant whatever they ask.

This book's prayers are in accord with the Word of God and will empower the church to walk according to the Holy Spirit and bring us victory in every domain in life.

It is a divine and a revolutionary task to safeguard this lost generation for eternal security in the hand of the Lord Jesus Christ and his Holy Father.

Boundless Prosperity will help its readers reap mighty financial harvests if they read it and practice its principles of financial prosperity. This book is meant to cause global spiritual revival and defeat the work of evil.

This book contains an overflow of godly prayers that will ensure that the people of God overcome every trouble and, especially, financial and spiritual troubles. It will make sure that their salvation is secure. Children of God will witness victory over everything during their lives in this world and the next.

The Lord Jesus Christ will come again and give us eternal redemptive bodies for our souls and spirits. When that happens, we will reign with the Lord in boundless prosperity forever in his glorious kingdom.

Now it is time to start calling on God, praising him, crying to him as did Enoch, the first to devotedly call on God; Yahweh took him to heaven alive.

Yahweh has and will always joyfully act and react favorably to faithful relationships that are based on faithful prayer.

CHAPTER 10
Prayer Sets

Part 1

Therefore I tell you, whatever you ask for in prayer, believe that you have received it, and it will be yours. (Mark 11:24)

Prayer Set 1

Holy Father, give me grace and favor to raise wisely my children in godly fear of you. Mal1

Anoint my soul to hate divorce. Empower me to lead my family in godly ways in fear of you and to be wise and prudent in avoiding the wickedness in this world. Mal2

Empower me to be always faithful with my tithing and offerings from every financial resource that comes into my hands for my church with a bold commitment. Mal3

Stop the terror of my enemies on my life. Ps10

Do not let me fall victim to my adversaries. Ps10

Eliminate their deceitful agenda and evil activity against me. Ps10

Wipe out the affliction that evildoers have brought over my life. Ps10

Do not let me be crushed by forces stronger than I. Ps10

In the name of the Lord Jesus Christ I pray.

Prayer Set 2

Holy Father, give me the wisdom to boldly and quickly refuse the advice and the temptation of the kingdom of darkness. Ma1

Give me the prudence and deep insight to successfully overcome the temptation and the tribulation from the kingdom of wickedness. Ma2

Provide me spiritual healing and strength to resist temptation and confusion in the invisible realm and in this world. Ma3

Show me clearly with great insight and wisdom all the wicked practices of the world and their source—the kingdom of darkness. Ma4

Give me grace, favor, humility, and a pure conscience to confess and repent all my wrongdoings. Ma5

Empower me to reject boldly everything that opposes your holy instructions and the leadership of the Holy Spirit in me. Ma6

Empower me to use well and productively the perfect gifts you give me to do your good work. Ma7

In the name of the Lord Jesus Christ I pray.

Prayer Set 3

Holy Father, show me how to produce a harvest of souls for salvation in your beloved Son Jesus Christ to bring into your holy kingdom. Ma8

Give me the grace and favor to never be angry at anyone. Ma11

Provide me the resources and wisdom to produce mighty financial harvests for your glory. De46

Prepare my mind and heart to avoid angry attitudes, expressions, and gestures when I am dealing with a bully or a nag. Ma12

Teach me and inspire me how to never look at anyone lustfully. Ma13

Anoint my eyes and my mind to look at anyone in a godly way. Ma14

Give me the wisdom to pray for people who are persecuting me. Ma15

Teach me and inspire me how to love my enemies the same way you love everybody. Ma16

In the name of the Lord Jesus Christ I pray.

Prayer Set 4

Holy Father, empower me to keep completely discreet my giving to others. Ma17

Heal my soul and my heart, and prepare me to forgive those who unfairly offend me. Ma18

Show me how to store up my treasures in your heavenly kingdom. Ma19

Heal my eyes, and teach me to keep them pure so my soul can shine with your glorious light. Ma20

Show me how to successfully seek your holy kingdom and practice its principles. Ma21

Empower me to never be anxious about anything in life. Rekindle my patience, hope, and trust in you. Ma22

In the name of the Lord Jesus Christ I pray.

Prayer Set 5

Holy Father, rest your mighty hand on me so I can proclaim your unshaking loving-kindness and your salvation to the ends of the earth. Ps30

Do not let me be entertained by ungodly worldly activity. Ps30

Give me victory over the slandering of my foes. Ps30

Let me rely on you to bring to you my request in times of adversity and needs. Ps30

Teach me not to judge others when they are not living according to your holy Word; show me how to be compassionate to them and show them patience, love, and kindness. Ma23

Give me your wisdom to know how to deal with people who are not willing to receive your salvation and instructions. Ma24

Provide me with the wisdom and determination to faithfully knock on your door in my times of need. Ma25

Show me how to seek you properly and find favor and mercy at your throne. Ma26

In the name of the Lord Jesus Christ I pray.

Prayer Set 6

Holy Father, let the fear of you remain bold in my soul so I will hate evil and enjoy doing what is right and honorable. Ma28

Give me a passion for loving, listening to, and learning your holy Word and instruction and to have bold courage to put them into practice always. Ma29

Anoint my heart and mind to love you more and above everyone and everything in this world. Ma31

Give me the strength and endurance to follow you and to bear my cross joyfully and without grumbling. Ma32

Motivate me to always make the right decision in choosing the life you have for me instead of my personal dreams. Ma33

Empower me to always and joyfully give a sizeable amount of my financial resources to support those who are serving you in ministry. Ma34

In the name of the Lord Jesus Christ I pray.

Prayer Set 7

Holy Father, heal my ears so I can hear your voice and identify right from wrong, and pour your salve on my eyes so I can see your holy path and not fall into darkness. Ma35

Let your holy Word take deep root in me so I can produce fruits of righteousness that greatly please you. Ma36

Empower me to boldly rely more on the pleasure from your holy presence in me. Ma37

Embolden my trust and hope in you immensely to wipe away the anxiety in my soul. Ma37

Give me the grace and favor to make your precepts and instructions my top priority above everything else in this world. Ma38

Show me all the great blessings you gladly plan to give me while in the presence of your holy people who gather in true unity of heart and spirit to pray and worship you.

In the name of the Lord Jesus Christ I pray.

Prayer Set 8

Holy Father, let me always be quick to forgive everyone who unfairly harms my soul. Ma41

Give me the wisdom to godly use wealth so I can acquire also the treasure of heaven. Ma44

Teach me to humble myself in communication and in leadership abilities.

Empower the church everywhere to make disciples as your beloved Son commanded his disciples after his resurrection. Ma45

Teach me to become a fully accomplished disciple who effectively works for your holy kingdom in taking your salvation to the lost people in the world.

Let discipleship become a practical priority again in all the churches today as in the time of the Lord Jesus and the apostolic era, when everyone in the church preached the gospel everywhere.

Humble me so I can joyfully obey your holy Word. 49

In the name of the Lord Jesus Christ I pray.

Prayer Set 9

Holy Father, deliver me from all my distress. Ps4

Bring relief to my soul from the troubles I am enduring. Ps4

Manifest your kindness to me by hearing my prayer. Ps4

Give me the grace and favor to be fully an accomplished disciple so I can do the godly work you set for me to do in holiness. Lu1

Empower me with the humility and grace to sincerely acknowledge to you my sins with sincere confession and repentance and to have the courage to accept your forgiveness. Lu2

Help me not take for granted the graceful presence of the Holy Spirit in me. Lu3

Let me always take refuge in you when I do not have the strength to do your work. Ps34

Empower me to walk holy before you. Ps34

In the name of the Lord Jesus Christ I pray.

Prayer Set 10

Holy Father, give me a permanent anointing to boldly hope in you and expect your promises. Ps37

Vanquish any angry attitude in my life. Ps37

Allow a stream of meekness to flow through my character like a mighty river. Ps37

Empower my soul to bless and honor your holy people everywhere. Ps37

Motivate me to always seek and pursue peace gently with wisdom among everyone. Ps37

Give me the grace to always take refuge in you in my times of need and distress. Ps37

Enlighten my heart and desire to prioritize your ordinances and your priorities from your special command. Ps37

Empower me with self-motivation and strength to lovingly obey the teaching of your beloved Son Jesus Christ passionately. Joh1

Give me the grace and favor to be sanctified in this world and empower me to be holy through the practice of your holy Word. Joh2

Heal my eyes with your salve so I can see your path, and lead me to the path that leads to success, holiness, eternal life, and superabundant prosperity. Joh4

In the name of the Lord Jesus Christ I pray.

Prayer Set 11

Holy Father, counsel me how to be in your presence when I reach the end of my life on earth. Ps49

Give me the grace to worship you with your holy angels in your holy kingdom after I reach the end of my life on earth. Ps49

Teach me to use your blessings for your glory when my cup is running over with your abundant, prosperous blessings. Ps49

Open my eyes to clearly see that obedience to your holy Word is the true riches that I need to rely on. Ps49

Anoint me to be joyfully excited by the awesomeness of your holy Word. Ps49

Empower me for a lifetime commitment in submission to the practices of your holy apostles in scripture to persevere every day in prayer and in the work you command me to do. Ac2

Give me the grace and favor to powerfully speak your Word with boldness, clarity, miraculous power, truth, and love so others can come to your salvation. Ac4

Empower me to repent and thus enable the fire of the Holy Spirit to remain always strong in me. Ac5

Remind me to always prioritize in my life prayer and the ministry you have given me so I can efficiently follow the guidance of the Holy Spirit. Ac6

In the name of the Lord Jesus Christ I pray.

Prayer Set 12

Holy Father, increase the fear of the Lord in my life every day.

Rain the river of unity, love, and tolerance in the hearts and minds of political parties in my country who do not share the same social and political ideology so they can work productively together respectfully according to your Word. Ac9

Let me be fully aware of the spiritual gifts you give me in the Lord Jesus Christ, and empower me with strength and wisdom to use them mightily for your glory. Ac10

Show me how to be a champion in helping and supporting the poor with everything you give me. Ac11

Give me a heart to boldly commit to prayer every day so the power of the Holy Spirit can help me to successfully do your good work and live a holy life. Ac12

Teach me to listen to the voice of the Holy Spirit in me so I can be a more efficient servant for your glory. Ac13

Show me how to fully understand and to practice the gospel of the kingdom as apostle Paul preached it, and empower me to teach it also every time you give me the opportunity to do so. Ac14

In the name of the Lord Jesus Christ I pray.

Part 2

Lord, who may dwell in your sacred tent? (Psalm 15:1)

Prayer Set 13

Holy Father, empower me to avoid the path of wickedness. Ps1

Motivate me not to enjoy the wickedness of ungodly people. Ps1

Help me to always forsake the club of immorality. Ps1

Teach me to take delight in your precepts. Ps1

Let my life abide in you to receive your blessing and water my land to make it fertile.

Allow my life to bring forth spiritual and financial productivity for your glory. Ps1

Empower me to obey your instructions in a smooth way and to rejoice in them. Ps1

Lead me to the way of uprightness. Ps1

In the name of the Lord Jesus Christ I pray.

Prayer Set 14

Holy Father, deliver me from those who conspire against me and those who plot to make me fail in life. Ps2

Break the cord and the chain that the power of wickedness uses to bind my soul.

Rebuke the spirits of darkness that pursue me, and terrify them with your anger. Ps2

Teach me to proclaim your decrees so others may know you better. Ps2

Let me live the prosperous inheritance you have written for me. Ps2

Empower me to defend myself from the kingdom of darkness when it plans to plunder my blessings. Ps2

Teach me to be wise and prudent in managing the spiritual and material gifts you provide me. Ps2

Let me serve you with fear and exalt your holy Word joyfully. Ps2

Remind me always to take refuge and delight in you. Ps2

In the name of the Lord Jesus Christ I pray.

Prayer Set 15

Holy Father, give me the wisdom to understand scripture and increase your fear and love in me to joyfully and seriously put your Word into practice. 2Tim1

Transform my heart and mind to hate wickedness and all ungodly activity in this world and to stay away from those who practice it. 2Tim2

Deliver me from all my foes who say you will not deliver me. Ps3

Be a shield around me, and lift me up high above my enemies. Sustain me in time of vulnerabilities. Ps3

Let my trust remain in you when my adversaries assail me. Ps3

Break their weapons of destruction, and deliver me from them all. Ps3

Let my blessings remain secure in your mighty hand. Ps3

In the name of the Lord Jesus Christ I pray.

Prayer Set 16

Holy Father, anoint me to love you more and more every day and to hate the wickedness in this world. Ps4

Empower me to be always faithful, and let me devote my life boldly to you. Ps4

Give me a heart and a strong desire to hate sin. Ps4

Let my body and life be a living sacrifice to you, and let me always trust in you. Ps4

Shower me with your abundant prosperity. Ps4

Provide me the resources and wisdom I need to produce financial harvests for your glory. De46

Shine your peaceful and protecting light on me. Ps4

Let your joy remain abundantly in my heart, and show me how to multiply my finances. Ps4

Let my life be in security everywhere under your protecting wings. Ps4

In the name of the Lord Jesus Christ I pray.

Prayer Set 17

Holy Father, empower and motivate me to hate wickedness. Ps5

Teach me to not welcome evil and evil people in my life and house. Ps5

Help me be humble all the time. Ps5

Give me your grace to love to do right and to practice righteous deeds always. Ps5

Empower me to use my body well as the house of the Holy Spirit. Ps5

Show me how to be humble before the Holy Spirit and be virtuous in everything. Ps5

Manifest your uprightness through my behavior, desire, and life. Ps5

Make your way clear and easy for me to follow. Ps5

In the name of the Lord Jesus Christ I pray.

Prayer Set 18

Holy Father, let me boldly acknowledge when I am walking on a wrong path. Ps6

Let me walk uprightly and rejoice in your presence. Ps6

Deliver me from your wrath, which distresses my soul. Ps6

Show me the way that leads to deliverance and healing. Ps6

Empower me to exalt you in good and bad times in sickness and in health. Ps6

Give me the favor and wisdom to bring wicked people to true repentance so they can receive salvation. Ps6

Pour a rain of spiritual blessing and financial harvest over my life so I can invest more in your good work. Ps6

Blot out the presence of evilness and evildoers in my life and house. Ps6

Answer this prayer speedily because of your unfailing love. Ps6

In the name of the Lord Jesus Christ I pray.

Prayer Set 19

Holy Father, teach me to bring honor and glory to you and seek you with all my heart. Ps4

Instruct me how not to entertain false gods or delight in them. Ps4

Deliver me from the kingdom of darkness, which always plots to destroy me. Ps7

Be my refuge and shield. Ps7

Restore to me everything my adversary has stolen for me and my country. Ps7

Pay attention to my prayers, cries, and laments. Ps5

Help me wait expectantly for your answer and your deliverance. Ps5

In the name of the Lord Jesus Christ I pray.

Prayer Set 20

Holy Father, manifest the majesty of your name through my life to the ends of the earth. Ps8

Let your glory be revealed through my life. Ps8

Empower me to silence your foes who trouble my life. Ps8

Establish me as a mighty stronghold against your enemies everywhere. Ps8

Be mindful of and responsive to my prayers. Ps8

Bless and empower me to do your work and conquer everything you put under my feet. Ps8

Receive this prayer with your unfailing love and tender mercy. Ps8

In the name of the Lord Jesus Christ I pray.

Prayer Set 21

Holy Father, do not let the wicked and corrupt triumph over me. Ps9

Give me a mind, heart, and desire to praise you always. Ps9

Deliver me from my enemies so I can exalt you with prayers of thanksgiving.

Do not let the wicked and the arrogant reign over me. Ps9

Cause the power of evil to turn back, stumble, and perish before me. Ps9

Give me victory toward my righteous cause and sovereign right. Ps9

Be my refuge and fortress from my oppressors. Ps9

Let me always put my trust in you and proclaim your wonders, salvation, and goodness to everyone. Ps9

Deliver your holy people and vulnerable citizen from the abuse and injustice of the realm of darkness and abusive human institutions. Ps9

In the name of the Lord Jesus Christ I pray.

Prayer Set 22

Holy Father, do not let me fall in the hand of my enemies and destroy all the equipment they use to bring me down. Ps10

Vanquish their ambushes and bring in public spectacle their conspiracy against me. Ps10

Let my plunderers and destroyers fail fall into their own traps and deliver me from their threats. Ps10

Let their evil ways be unfruitful and sterile. Ps10

Vanquish their plan when they sneer at me. Ps10

Bring down the pride of the wicked who torment my soul. Ps10

Let humility be manifest in all aspects of my life. Ps10

Do not let arrogant, wicked people trample me. Ps10

In the name of the Lord Jesus Christ I pray.

Prayer Set 23

Holy Father, empower me to avoid foolish talk, ungodly jokes, and indecent behavior and clothing. Ep10

Empower me to make the most of my time every day in praying, reading scripture, and supporting others who need help and diligently work for your glory. Ep11

Embolden your love in my soul and give me the grace to manifest it to everyone and especially my spouse and children. Ep12

Bless me to devotedly rejoice in you daily through songs of praise and worship with thanksgiving from the psalms, hymns, and cantic. 13

Let my foundation be well grounded in you for life. Ps11

Be my shield and fortress when my adversary secretly shoots his arrows at me. Ps11

Destroy their evil weapons and let their sharp arrows turn far away from me. Ps11

In the name of the Lord Jesus Christ I pray.

Prayer Set 24

Holy Father, restore everything plunderers have taken from me. Ps12

Bring loyal people to me to help me carry out the destiny you have for me. Ps12

Empower me to be humble in speech and strengthen my tongue to always speak truthfully, prudently, and with wisdom. Ps12

Bless me to restore the poor who have been unfortunate in life. Ps12

Let me be always aware that you are near me and that your eyes never leave sight of me. Ps 10

Rescue me and lift me up in time of difficulty. Ps10

In the name of the Lord Jesus Christ I pray.

Part 3

Your mercy, O Lord, is in the heavens; your faithfulness reaches to the clouds. (Psalm 36:5 NKJV)

Prayer Set 25

Holy Father, increase in me your wisdom to always live boldly in full maturity and to apply your holy instructions. Pr1

Let me use your wisdom prudently and humbly in receiving your instructions. Pr2

Empower me to honor prudence and discretion in practicing your knowledge and wisdom from my activities in this world every day in my relationships with others. Pr3

Teach me to avoid foolishness and arrogance. Pr4

Let me never mock your holy Word and instructions. Pr5

Anoint my heart and mind to joyfully and humbly receive your rebuke or discipline and to love listening to your advice and knowledge. Pr6

In the name of the Lord Jesus Christ I pray.

Prayer Set 26

Holy Father, do not let my enemies overwhelm me with shame when I walk uprightly before you. Ps25

Help me live with integrity. Ps25

Protect and deliver me when I am afflicted by distress and when people slander me without cause. Ps25

Save me from the traps and ambushes of my foes. Ps25

Empower me to manage my live and business discreetly and bless me with understanding of your words and instructions so I can please you always. Pr7

Empower me to manage my resources in a manner that brings productivity for your holy kingdom and protect my resources with your fiery shield. Pr8

Empower me with wisdom and prudence to avoid sexual immorality. Pr9

In the name of the Lord Jesus Christ I pray.

Prayer Set 27

Holy Father, empower me to keep your holy wisdom alive in my activities. Pr10

Prepare me to always provide for those in need when I can. Pr11

Provide me the resources and wisdom to produce financial harvests for your glory. De46

Uphold me and give me the grace to be blameless for my activities and bless my house. Pr12

Motivate me to always bring honor to you as my first fruit. Pr13

Show me to never be wise in my own eyes. Pr14

Show me to practice your love fully and make it a priority in my life. Pr15

In the name of the Lord Jesus Christ I pray.

Prayer Set 28

Holy Father, allow me to learn and love your wisdom and empower me to put that into practice.

Give me the grace and favor to understand your holy instruction. Pr15

Bless my mouth to avoid immoral and corrupted expression in conversation. Pr16

Increase in me your authority and wisdom to always overcome the temptation of sexual immorality, greed, and any corrupt practices against your holy Word. Pr17

Show me the negative effects of sexual immorality and disobedience to your Word. Pr18

Fill me with your love and joy by the presence of the Holy Spirit. Pr19

In the name of the Lord Jesus Christ I pray.

Prayer Set 29

Holy Father, pour into my soul abundant energy and strength to do your work tirelessly. Pr20

Give me a strong desire to detest boastfulness, despise lying and evil practices, and dislike creating dissension. Pr21

Give me self-discipline in working diligently for abundant productivity. Pr22

Inspire me to wisely deal with mockers and upright people alike. Pr23

Anoint me to be wise regarding making decisions based on the guidance and counsel of the Holy Spirit. Pr24

Empower my hand to be diligent and productive to better establish your good work everywhere. Pr25

Anoint me and empower me to walk righteously before you. Pr26

Show me how to joyfully obey your Word through your holy instructions. Pr27

In the name of the Lord Jesus Christ I pray.

Prayer Set 30

Holy Father, let your holy Word guide my heart through the counsel of your Holy Spirit so I can be successful in everything. Pr28

Renew your anointing in my mind to be kind in heart, speech, and attitude. Pr29

Teach me not to speak rashly, and give me the wisdom to guard my speech. Pr30

Empower me to encourage others for your glory. Pr31

Let the answer from my mouth be kind when others criticize me. Pr32

Teach me to make your ways the pleasure of my life. Pr33

Empower me to passionately seek the understanding of your Word and instructions. Pr34

Motivate me to successfully walk faithfully and prudently. Pr35

In the name of the Lord Jesus Christ I pray.

Prayer Set 31

Holy Father, anoint my heart to be wise and my mouth to proclaim what is true and just. Pr39

Empower me to have great fear of you in everything I do and think. Pr40

Provide me profoundly great insight, knowledge, and wisdom to lead successfully my house and my work. Pr41

Give me the grace and favor to never be wise in my own eyes especially in times of prosperity. Pr42

Humble my soul with your grace to confess sincerely and truthfully my wrongdoings, and empower me to repent of my sins. Pr43

Teach me to speak calmly and in full control of myself. Ps44

Empower me to remain always in humility of heart and spirit. Pr45

Let me always seek your presence for happiness, joy, and contentment bur never in alcoholic beverages, cigarette, drugs, and all worldly entertainment. Pr46

Bless me to be a passionate advocate of the poor in upright speech and their supporter spiritually, logistically, academically, financially, and regarding their health. Pr47

In the name of the Lord Jesus Christ I pray.

Prayer Set 32

Holy Father, be my shield from those who plan to shame my private and public lives. Ps31

Remind me to bring my cry to you and keep my eyes on you. Ps31

Give me a heart and mind that detests idolatry and isolates me from all wickedness. Ps31

Motivate me to rededicate my devotion to you from time to time. Ps31

Provide me the strength and memory to bring my sorrows and distresses to you when others slander me. Ps31

Bless me to be a mighty blessing to all members of my close and remote families, and all people. Ps31

Motivate me to take the day of my death seriously, to meditate about it in godliness, and to make righteous preparation in a manner that pleases you. Ec1

Teach me to practice wisdom and righteousness moderately, not in excess, in a way that does not harm me or others. Ec2

Give me a bold devotion to serving you and a humble attitude that pleases you always. Ec3

In the name of the Lord Jesus Christ I pray.

Prayer Set 33

Holy Father, let your will prosper in my life, and empower me to bring a multitude of people to salvation. Is1

Let me always take refuge in you; create on my lips songs of praise and exaltation to you with thanksgiving because you are worthy of praise. Is2

Bless me and motivate me how to feed and shelter the poor and give them hope of your love through the salvation of your beloved Son. Is3

Empower my ear to listen attentively and clearly to your instructions so I can always please you in holy living. Is5

Let your glory be seen in my life in uprightness through the spiritual gifts you give me. Is7

In the name of the Lord Jesus Christ I pray.

Prayer Set 34

Holy Father, pour your anointing of the peaceful and loving power of the Holy Spirit on me and my posterity for generations. Is8

Rekindle your blessed promises to me and extend them to my posterity. Is9

Let your river from your holy throne flow on my fruitless land to water and fertilize my ground to produce mighty spiritual and financial harvests at all times. Is10

Waken my soul and spirit early in the morning so I can bring songs of praise to you and present my prayers and petitions with thanksgiving so your power can be fruitful and clearly be seen in my life. Is11

Save my children from all ungodly practices and wicked entertainment that bring spiritual confusion to their minds. Is12

Empower my soul to peacefully rejoice in you with songs of thanksgiving and praise. Is13

In the name of the Lord Jesus Christ I pray.

Prayer Set 35

Holy Father, break the yoke of poverty off my neck and erase the ungodly thoughts and negative habits from my life when I was a slave of my sinful flesh. Je1

Despoil the plunderers of my resources and restore everything they have stolen from me seven times more. Je2

Bring honor to the good work you have entrusted me to do as I honor you by doing your work on earth. Je3

Let my spiritual calling be fruitful as you dwell in my soul and lead me. Je4

Let me and my posterity rejoice through the blessings you give us. Je5

Show me and my posterity how to avoid others in the ministry who will make the spiritual gifts you provide us useless. Je6

Show me and my posterity how to be content in godliness with the earthly abundant resources you provide us. Je7

Turn always our sorrows into a stream of gladness and peace with your glorious and joyful presence in us. Je8

In the name of the Lord Jesus Christ I pray.

Prayer Set 36

Holy Father, let my words be truthful and sincere. Ps5

Let my heart be pure and without malice, and let my mouth praise you always. Ps5

Deliver me from my sinful behavior, and let your hand lift me up from my downfall. Ps5

Free my soul from the conspiracy of my enemies. Ps5

Destroy the negative impact of my sins, and empower me to use these experiences to better myself. Ps5

Let all the nations be aware of your sovereignty and the immensity of your power through creation to bring forth in their hearts exceeding fear of you. J11

Restore fully in my storehouse the wealth the enemy has stolen from me and my ancestors. J12

In the name of the Lord Jesus Christ I pray.

Part 4

Holy, Holy, Holy, is the LORD of hosts, the whole earth is full of His glory. (Isaiah 6:3 ESV)

Prayer Set 37

Holy Father, instruct me how to always keep ablaze the fire of the Holy Spirit in me and to teach it to others. 1Thes16

Empower me to never have as friends people who reject your instructions. 1Thes18

Give me endurance and bold courage to never tire of doing good. 1Thes19

Let me triumph over my troubles because of your unfailing love. Ps13

Overwhelm my soul with your joy when my heart is sorrowful. Ps13

Manifest your shining light on me to bring peace and security in my soul. Ps13

Pay special attention to this prayer, and let your praise be forever on my lips. Ps13

In the name of the Lord Jesus Christ I pray.

Prayer Set 38

Holy Father, give me a heart and mind to humbly seek you every day in spirit and truth. Ps14

Help me live a holy and godly life. Ps14

Empower me to practice righteousness and do your work under your eyes. Ps14

Provide me with the resources and wisdom to produce a mighty financial harvest for your glory. De46

Lead me to stay on your holy path and to live justly. Ps14

Instruct me how to call you and to receive from you better so I can bring multitudes to salvation. Ps 14

Teach me to live holy in this world of corruption. Ps14

Manifest your glory on me so people can be encouraged to serve you. Ps14

In the name of the Lord Jesus Christ I pray.

Prayer Set 39

Holy Father, empower me to honor those who fear you; remind me to stay away from those who practice wickedness. Ps15

Teach me to keep my oath even when it hurts to do so. Ps15

Remind me to lend money to the poor without interest. Ps15

Empower me to never accept bribes.

Let my life be blameless before you, and motivate me to do what is right. Ps15

Empower me to speak the truth from my heart and never slander others. Ps15

Teach me to always please your Holy Spirit so he can joyfully dwell in me. Ps15

Let my faith be unshakeable in you, and motivate me to always look up to you on your holy throne. Ps15

In the name of the Lord Jesus Christ I pray.

Prayer Set 40

Holy Father, teach me to be prudent in using the names of people who go after other gods. Ps16

Give me the wisdom to cause my blessings to be fully protected under your mighty wings every day. Ps16

Let my land and my financial blessings be on pleasant and secure places. Ps16

Let me explore and acquire the full inheritance you have set aside for me according to your Word. Ps16

Teach me to keep my eyes always on you. Ps16

Give me the wisdom of how to take great delight in you among your righteous people. Ps16

Favor me to live a life that brings pleasure to you always. Ps16

Let me strongly depend on your joyful presence, and let my tongue praise you gladly. Ps16

In the name of the Lord Jesus Christ I pray.

Prayer Set 41

Holy Father, protect me from all who conspire to destroy me. Ps17

Deliver me from those who are taking bribes to plunder my resources and vanquish my life. Ps17

Protect my sovereign right wonderfully, and pour special blessings on me to be a conqueror in this world. Ps17

Open my mouth to speak what is right. Ps17

Vanquish the plot of my enemies and their coercive presence on my territory. Ps17

Empower my eyes to follow your path so I will not fall in the pit of the ungodly. Ps17

Let no evil be in my heart. Ps17

Vindicate me in the presence of the unjust rules of those stronger than me. Ps17

Blot out my enemies' plans to plunder my resources. Ps17

Protect my sovereign right every day from all my enemies. Ps17

In the name of the Lord Jesus Christ I pray.

Prayer Set 42

Holy Father, deliver me from the cord of the wicked and all destruction. Ps18

Hear my voice from your holy temple in heaven. Ps18

Be angry with my enemies and their schemes; let the smoke of your nostrils consume their unjust and corrupt ways. Ps18

Shoot your arrows to disperse my adversaries and plunderers. Ps18

Expose their wickedness and cause their condemnation. Ps18

Take hold of me from your holy throne and confront those who oppose me without cause. Ps18

Save me from their haughtiness. Ps18

Let your shining face lighten my path so I can see where to go. Ps18

Arm me with strength and secure my path. Ps18

Do not let my opponent entrap me in my days of vulnerability. Ps18

Pursue my enemies from the realm of darkness and destroy them. Ps18

Give me victory over my slanderers. Ps18

Put me high above my adversaries. Ps18

Empower me to exalt you in private and public. Ps18

Bless me and my posterity to use our financial prosperity in a manner that pleases you. Ps18

In the name of the Lord Jesus Christ I pray.

Prayer Set 43

Holy Father, empower me to fully know you well, understand your Word, and obey you. Ps19

Give me the wisdom to apply your Word and prioritize your instructions. Ps19

Let my life shine as the sun to bring mighty spiritual revival to the ends of the world. Ps19

Manifest strongly your fear and ordinances forever in my soul. Ps19

Empower me to fully overcome my hidden sins and weaknesses. Ps19

Give the grace to abandon any willful sin. Ps19

In the name of the Lord Jesus Christ I pray.

Prayer Set 44

Holy Father, help me every day to triumph over the traps of the realm of darkness. Ps35

Put to shame false accusations my adversaries bring against me. Ps35

Change my distresses into a stream of joyfulness. Ps20

Protect me with your mighty wings and lift me up high from your holy throne. Ps20

Let me enter the fullness of my great destiny under your prosperous blessings so I can accomplish honorably the vision you have highlighted in my heart. Ps20

Let your holy vision for me be manifest in my life for your own glory. Ps20

Increase my trust in you every day. Ps20

In the name of my Lord Jesus Christ I pray.

Prayer Set 45

Holy Father, manifest more your glory in me when I am doing your work to attract multitudes for salvation. Ps20

Let your joy in me reach deep down into my soul. Ps20

Let my trust in you be unshakeable every day. Ps20

Quench the spirits of darkness with your mighty fire when they attack me. Ps20

Vanquish them from the ends of the earth. Ps20

Let the flow of my blessings be unstoppable under the security of your mighty hand. Ps20

Cause my enemies to be far away in the time of my deliverance, and let your sharp arrows attack them from all sides. Ps20

Give me the wisdom to never work with those who will cause my ruin. Ps20

Empower me to always praise and exalt you and show gratitude for your salvation. Ps20

Let my life be full of years with good health in uprightness to show your glory and loving-kindness. Ps20

In the name of my Lord Jesus Christ I pray.

Prayer Set 46

Holy Father, let my heart for you remain firm in times of adversity, and let my eyes rest on you until you show me compassion. Ps22

Remind me that your loving eyes will always remain on me to guide me to victory and success. Ps22

Give me strength to endure and overcome the deadly sword of my enemies. Ps22

Let my trust and hope remain joyfully strong in you when people slander me and bring irony to me in time of difficulties. Ps22

Remind me that you are in control of my life; remind me that your loving-kindness will never depart me. Ps22

Give me a tangible sign that you have heard my cry and the insurance that my answer is coming and will not be late. Ps22

Provide me wisdom and power to testify to how you have delivered me from impossible problems. Ps22

Do not let me be put to shame, and assure me you are not abandoning me. Ps22

In the name of my Lord Jesus Christ I pray.

Prayer Set 47

Holy Father, show me how to secure my financial resources under your wings when thieves come to plunder them. Ps23

Protect my anointed overflowing cups of blessings and my resources in my storehouses. Ps23

Empower me to obey your Word and obtain your abundant blessings. Ps23

Empower me to be holy in everything I do, think, and desire in this world of darkness and confusion. Ps23

Enlighten me to wisely know how to better come to you so I can better receive strength and your fresh anointing in times of need. Ps23

Protect me with your sharp sword and fierce arrows when the kingdom of darkness comes down to drive me into the pit of death. Ps23

Train me well to always please your Holy Spirit, who dwells in me. Ps23

Manifest your unfailing love, kindness, and favor in my life forever. Ps23

In the name of my Lord Jesus Christ I pray.

Prayer Set 48

Holy Father, give me a heart, strength, and mind to seek and praise you daily. Ps24

Let my voice reach your holy mountain. Ps24

Remove any deceit from my heart. Ps24

Let me work for your glory. Ps24

Vindicate me by the power of the cross from any judgment brought against me. Ps24

Open your floodgates of blessings and pour them continually over me. Ps24

In the name of my Lord Jesus Christ I pray.

Part 5

God is my refuge and strength. Psalm 46.1

Prayer Set 49

Holy Father, give me a heart and a humble attitude to obey you and not rebel against your commands. Ps5

Let me always take refuge in you. Ps5

Manifest your joy in me when I take refuge in you, and inspire in me new songs in my heart to joyfully praise you. Ps5

Let your shield surround me and multiply your favor to me. Ps5

Manifest your blessing to me every day. Ps5

Give me the favor and grace to embolden my commitment to serving you with all my mind and heart. De22

Restore to me all the enemy has stolen from me and my ancestors, and give me the wisdom to use them for your glory and support your work in the world. De23

In the name of the Lord Jesus Christ I pray.

Prayer Set 50

Holy Father, give me your grace and favor so my life is full of days, and multiply my posterity and empower them to live holy before you. De24

Protect us from the enemies' weapons and empower us to take authority over the realm of darkness and overcome their sea of temptation. De25

Bless the spiritual gifts and skills you give us to do your work and care for our families. De27

Provide me the resources and wisdom to produce mighty financial harvests for your glory. De46

Empower us to use our gifts and skills in a manner that pleases you greatly. De28

Nullify the power of the kingdom of darkness that is at work against us, and empower us to be prudent in the face of its destructive agenda. De29

In the name of the Lord Jesus Christ I pray.

Prayer Set 51

Holy Father, remind me that I am always secure under your mighty hand, and let my soul rest in your loving presence, unfailing love, and peace. De30

May the blessing that comes from your throne remain always on me and my posterity. De31

Show me how to productively and uprightly use the favors you provide me through the grace that provides salvation to humanity. De33

Empower me to rejoice in you from morning to night every day. De34

Teach us to use wisely the prosperity you give us so we can exalt you and proclaim your salvation. De35

Teach us to use what you provide to us to support your good work and your vulnerable people. De36

In the name of the Lord Jesus Christ I pray.

Prayer Set 52

Holy Father, give me and my posterity the favor and grace to have great success in our finances and in the good works you command us to do. De38

Give me the wisdom to proclaim judgment on the realm of darkness, which is causing terrible harm to your vulnerable people. De39

Let me and my posterity be full of your favor and grace to fulfill the fullness of our great destinies. De40

Let our business reflect the principle and manner of your kingdom and be lucrative in manifesting your glorious love and prosperity. De41

Give us the wisdom and prudence to deal peacefully with our enemies. De43

In the name of the Lord Jesus Christ I pray.

Prayer Set 53

Holy Father, give me grace so my deeds will be godly and perfect in your eyes. Re9

Embolden my conviction to keep putting your Word into practice, and humble me courageously to sincerely repent of my sins. Re10

Waken me with your holy anointing so I can follow you with attention and passion. Re11

Teach me to master every weakness in my sinful flesh so you can delight in mc always. Re12

Show me how to rely more on you as my only hope for everything. 13

Teach me to be enriched by your refined gold, to be clothed in white linen, and to let your light shine in me. Re14

Let your salve soothe my eyes so I can see your holy path and not fall into darkness. Re15

Give me the grace and favor to know all the steps and the mentality that bring people to fall into spiritual lukewarmness so I can know how to overcome them. Re16

Empower me to successfully avoid spiritual lukewarmness in this life. Re17

In the name of the Lord Jesus Christ I pray.

Prayer Set 54

Holy Father, empower me to be strong and courageous when I face adversity. Jo1

Give me the wisdom, courage, and patience to fight principalities, the powers of darkness, the leaders in the invisible world, and the harmful spirit in the celestial realm. Jo2

Help me remember all your instructions and words, and magnify my power to be attentive to your command to fight the fortresses in the invisible realm, which never stop attacking my soul and my mind. Jo3

Give me your wisdom and strength to submit joyfully to your Word. Jo4

Let your Word be in my speech for guidance and in my mind for meditation. Jo5

Show me how to keep always the fire of the Holy Spirit ablaze in my soul. Jo6

Remind me that you are with me always to erase the fear of loneliness and of evil spirits when I am alone, and empower me to be aware of your presence for comfort. Jo7

Give me the grace and favor to conquer every land and territory you set for me to possess. Jo8

In the name of the Lord Jesus Christ I pray.

Prayer Set 55

Holy Father, motivate my soul and mind to have zero tolerance for sin. Jo9

Show me how to bring the spirits of darkness to confusion and defeat when they gather to steal and destroy my blessings. Jo10

Give me the strength, courage, and wisdom to defeat the enemy. Jo11

Bless and empower me to renew my commitment to serve you better. Jo12

Give me the courage to move forward faithfully in the mighty hand of the Lord Jesus Christ. Ju13

Train me to be an accomplished and mighty warrior in your army. Ju14

Empower me to have the strength and wisdom to be a better soldier in your army. Ju15

In the name of the Lord Jesus Christ I pray.

Prayer Set 56

Holy Father, show me a path to recovery with no shame when people slander me because of my vulnerabilities and failures. Ps25

Blot out every shame spread over my live. Ps25

Let me be always stronger than my enemies. Ps25

Empower me to avoid the path that drives me to sin. Ps25

Do not let the prophetic and inspired words you put in my mouth fall on the floor. 1Sa1

Empower me with the wisdom to always ask you things I desire but not according to the sinful flesh. 1Sa3

Increase your fear and love in my mind and heart. 1Sa4

Increase your power in me to serve you faithfully. 1Sa5

In the name of the Lord Jesus Christ I pray.

Prayer Set 57

Holy Father, let me and my posterity increase in faith, uprightness, sanctification, and holiness. 2Sa1

Animate my spirit to receive all the blessings and territory you set aside for me to possess so I can magnify the power of your holy name. 2Sa2

Train and empower me daily to defeat the powers of darkness at work against me and your holy people. 2Sa3

Give me a bold humility to accept your and your qualified leaders' chastisement so I can receive healing and grow in faith. 2Sa4

Empower me to perfectly use every gift you give me to take care of my family and productively do your good works. 2Sa5

In the name of the Lord Jesus Christ I pray.

Prayer Set 58

Holy Father, instruct me perfectly how the blood of the Lord Jesus Christ wipes away the cursing power of the kingdom of darkness and sin in me. 2Sa6

Show me excellently how to take victorious authority over the cursing spirits in the kingdom of darkness every day. 2Sa7

Help me to learn your holy instruction in the Holy Scripture passionately. 2Sa8

Empower me to proclaim wisely your faithfulness and salvation to the ends of the world. 2Sa11

Show me how to use efficiently the authority you provide me in the Lord Jesus Christ so I can break every weapon of evilness and nullify their attacks on me. 2sa13

In the name of the Lord Jesus Christ I pray.

Prayer Set 59

Holy Father, create a smooth and secure path for me so I can avoid falling into the traps of the enemy. 2Sa15

Let all my enemies fall into their own traps. 2Sa16

Give me victory over the attacks of my foes, and let the world witness it. 2Sa17

Manifest your unfailing kindness and grace in me and my posterity, and allow us to be successful in everything that brings glory to you. 2Sa18

Empower me to devote my life to exalt and praise you in spirit and truth. 2Sa19

Give me the favor to lead my family in your fear and help them fulfill the calling you endow in their lives for your glory. 2Sa20

Give me the grace, favor, and power to be prudent and live with your fear so I will never provoke your anger or sadden the Holy Spirit in me. 2Sa21

In the name of the Lord Jesus Christ I pray.

Prayer Set 60

Holy Father, give me your grace for my house to be always in order, at peace, and in your love. 2Sa22

Bless my posterity to always live in fear of you, and give them the grace and favor to choose virtuous spouses who fear you. Ez23

Bless me to be a builder for your sacred work first among your holy servants and then everyone else. Ne24

Nullify the power of every entity that opposes my good work and financial productivity. Ne25

Instruct me how to reserve part of my possession and finances to help the poor everywhere. Ne26

Give me the wisdom and favor to prioritize the practice of your holy Word with all its instructions and the reading of the Bible daily to better obey you. Ne27

Give me the grace and favor to have as counselors and friends mature elders in the church in whom I can confide to help me walk holy before you. Ne28

In the name of the Lord Jesus Christ I pray.

Part 6

Nevertheless, I will bring health and healing to it; I will heal my people and will let them enjoy abundant peace and security. (Jeremiah 33:6)

Prayer Set 61

Holy Father, bring comfort to my soul by reminding me that all my sins are blotted out by the blood of the Lamb, your beloved Son. Ps25

Empower me to always humble myself before you in times of prayer and praise in private and in great assemblies. Ps25

Teach me to humble myself before every one every day. Ps25

Help me to successfully practice humility through all aspect of life. Ps25

Empower me to overcome the sins of my youth. Ps25

Let your way always be clear before me. Ps25

Instruct me how to faithfully walk with you. Ps25

Let me walk faithfully when my enemies are pushing me to go the opposite way. Ps25

Put me always above my enemies. Ps25

Let my life shine above my enemies so they can fear you and come to repentance. Ps25

Let your glory manifest and remain in my life so I can attract multitudes for salvation, healing, and deliverance. Ps25

In the name of my Lord Jesus Christ I pray.

Prayer Set 62

Holy Father, teach me to avoid the friendship of unfaithful people and from associating with immoral institutions. Ps26

Give me a perfect hatred of the institutions of evildoers. Ps26

Motivate me not to be in the company of the deceitful. Ps26

Let me not take for granted your merciful kindness and graceful blessings. Ps26

Show me how to depend only on you for everything. Ps26

Train my heart and mind to be without reproach before your eyes. Ps26

Lead me to faithfully use my body honorably as the temple of the Holy Spirit. Ps26

Teach me personally how to successfully please you through your holy Word. Ps26

Inspire me with the upright life of your beloved Son Jesus to do the work he entrusts me to do. Ps26

In the name of my Lord Jesus Christ I pray you.

Prayer Set 63

Holy Father, empower me to clearly see your goodness and kindness through my life, others, and throughout all your creation. Ps27

Give me the strength to patiently wait of your promises and to also boldly expect of their accomplishment. Ps27

May your light and the power of your salvation manifest through my soul to be a stronghold around me from the attack of my adversaries. Ps27

Bring down my enemies with the power of the Holy Spirit. Ps27

Anoint me to seek your face as a refuge at any time. Ps27

Exalt my head above all my enemies. Ps27

Let my soul find comfort and security from your holy mountain. Ps27

Overwhelm my soul with the joy of your beloved Son Jesus Christ when I am seeking your face. Ps27

Let your presence comfort me when everyone forsakes me. Ps27

Cause your way to be smooth and easy when I am fulfilling your holy work. Ps27

Do not let me fall because of the will of my enemies. Ps27

In the name of my Lord Jesus Christ I pray.

Prayer Set 64

Holy Father, motivate me every day to not participate in or associate with the activities of wicked people. Ps28

Let justice be in my land and bring judgment up on those who continue to plunder your vulnerable people. Ps28

Keep me away from those who willfully oppose to obey your holy Word. Ps28

Give me a clear and a bold way to stay far away from those who enjoy wickedness. Ps28

Let me always cry to you for help, and motivate me to depend on you always as the principal source of my security and strength. Ps28

Deliver me from my weaknesses, and rain your blessings on me. Ps28

Give me victory over my work, and lift me above my enemies. Ps28

Provide me the resources and wisdom to produce a mighty financial harvest for your glory. De46

Let your ear be attentive to my petitions and answer all my requests. Ps28

In the name of my Lord Jesus Christ I pray.

Prayer Set 65

Holy Father, let your Word enlighten my soul so I can be an example and a reference for your people, who are looking for direction. Ps29

Let your Word be powerful lighting in my life so multitudes can be free of the chain of evilness.

Let your holy Word in my speech destroy iniquity and darkness in others' lives. Ps29

Motivate me to work tirelessly and never weary for the glory of your kingdom. Ps29

Empower me to express your Word to put evildoers and the realm of darkness to shame. Ps29

Permit your Word to bring forth fruit of righteousness in my life for your glory. Ps29

Rain the wisdom of your holy Word on my family and me to bring lasting peace. Ps29

In the name of my Lord Jesus Christ I pray.

Prayer Set 66

Holy Father, prepare me to testify in private and in public to the many awesome miracles you have done for me, my family, and others. Ps30

Vanquish my weaknesses that isolate me from you. Ps30

Destroy the attacks of wicked spirits on my family and me. Ps30

Empower my mouth and mind to praise you every day. Ps30

Teach me to learn your Word in fear and humility so you can rejoice in my devotion to you. Ps30

Enlighten me to look for your favor every day. Ps30

Empower me to rely on your joy and seek it when I am in distress. Ps30

Manifest your love and security through the shining light of the spirit of truth in my heart. Ps30

Give me the maturity to conquer evil spirits and people who try to chain me in the shadow of death. Ps30

Transform my lamentation into gladness in times of distress. Ps30

In the name of my Lord Jesus Christ I pray.

Prayer Set 67

Holy Father, cause me not to be isolated from your holy people. Ps31

Bless me also with mighty prayer warriors who live uprightly and help me fulfill the Great Commission. Ps31

Isolate my enemies from the work you have called me, and vanquish my existence from their memory. Ps31

Enchain my adversaries. Ps31

Let my adversaries be put to shame, and empower me to lead them to repent of their wicked ways. Ps31

Bless me to bring to shame the prideful and the arrogant according to your Word. Ps31

Manifest your goodness and favor in my family and me in the sight of all. Ps31

Manifest your unfailing love to me in times of adversity. Ps31

Anoint me to be true to you at all times. Ps31

In the name of my Lord Jesus Christ I pray you.

Prayer Set 68

Holy Father, show me how to work better on the plan of prosperity and uprightness you have written for me so I can be productive for the Great Commission. Ps33

Let the fear of you abide strongly in my heart to please you always. Ps33

Manifest your lordship to bring spiritual revival, justice, peace, and prosperity to my family and country. Ps33

Anoint me to have a bold fear of you and always be a person of integrity before your eyes. Ps33

Give me a strong love to meditate on and obey your holy Word always. Ps33

Empower me to exalt and honor you lovingly and respectably. Ps33

In the name of my Lord Jesus Christ I pray.

Prayer Set 69

Holy Father, let me be aware that you are near to comfort me when my spirit is in distress and my heart is in anguish. Ps34

Remind me that you are seriously paying attention to my cries in prayer. Ps43

Motivate me to always seek peace and pursue it everywhere. Ps34

Empower me to pursue and seek your kingdom and live by its principles and culture. Ps34

Empower me to speak uprightly and truthfully at all times. Ps43

Let me pay full attention to your counsel. Ps34

Let your fear be strong in my spirit and my heart forever. Ps34

Let your praise be always on my lips. Ps34

Empower me to bring your people to boldly praise you in spirit and truth with all their heart. Ps34

In the name of my Lord Jesus Christ I pray.

Prayer Set 70

Holy Father, secure my life and blessings from the devil's conspiracy to plunder my resources and destroy my life. Ps35

Favor me with your grace to explore all the riches and assets you have for me. Ps35

Stop, Lord, the plundering of the realm of darkness over my life, and bring back seven times everything they have stolen from me. Ps35

Vanquish the authority of the realm of darkness over me and my country. Ps35

Empower me to praise and thank you through new songs for deliverance from those too strong from me. Ps35

Let the powers of darkness be entrapped in the snares they have set for me. Ps35

Break the arrows of my adversaries when they persecute me without cause, and do not allow them to execute their plans to impoverish me. Ps35

Defend me with the power of your right and your right hand. Ps35

Anoint me to exalt you because of your unfailing love and your awesome power. Ps35

In the name of my Lord Jesus Christ I pray.

Prayer Set 71

Holy Father, protect me from the power of arrogant people. Ps36

Give me strength to stay on your path when the winds of evil come. Ps36

Anoint my heart and mind to always hate sin and to isolate myself from them when they come my way. Ps36

Give me the gift of humility in speech and action. Ps36

Provide me wisdom to study my previous ways that brought me to sin so I can overcome iniquity. Ps36

Empower me to act wisely and walk uprightly in your sight. Ps36

Give me the courage and humility to abandon every wrongful and sinful path. Ps36

Give me a strong desire to never meditate evil against people. Ps36

Strengthen my heart, bless my finances, and direct my path to do the wonderful and majestic work you entrust me to do. Ps36

Anoint me to expect your promises and blessings you pronounce over my life. Ps36

Empower me to bring wicked and arrogant people to repentance. Ps36

In the name of my Lord Jesus Christ I pray.

Prayer Set 72

Holy Father, forgive me for not praying to you enough as the Bible teaches. Show me clearly how not to forsake you, my first love. Re1

Empower me to create enough quality time in prayer for everything especially concerning the work you entrusted to me. 2

Empower me to study the practices of the Nicolaitans so I can learn to hate them as you do and to avoid them. Re3

Show me how to have bold courage to overcome persecution even to the point of death. Re4

Instruct me of the teaching of Balaam and how it is practiced in the world so I can avoid and warn others of it. Re5

Train me to have bold victory to reject always the ways of the Nicolaitans and Balaam. Re6

Instruct me well in the doctrine of the prophet Jezebel and the destructive effect of her teaching on churches. Re7

Show me better how to overcome Jezebel's teaching. Re8

In the name of my Lord Jesus Christ I pray.

Part 7
Lord Jesus Christ Walks on Water (John 6:16–21)

Prayer Set 73

Holy Father, give my children the grace and favor to be obedient to your holy Word and to pursue holiness and sanctification all their lives. 2Tim9

Give me your grace and favor to live holy and to love you with all my heart and mind. 2Tim10

Motivate me to prioritize praising and worshipping you forever. Ps146

Increase my trust in you and eliminate my trust in people. Ps146

Bless me abundantly to care for vulnerable people specifically in countries where they are deprived of their right to work, go to school, receive public health care, and be treated as equal persons. Ps146

Embolden my hope and expectation in your promises and salvation. Ps146

In the name of the Lord Jesus Christ I pray.

Prayer Set 74

Holy Father, anoint me to live a life of integrity in your sight.

Put me high among your people; let my life be honored to the ends of the earth. Ps38

With your tender mercy and graceful favor, direct my path and cause my life to be respected everywhere. Ps38

Let my speech and manners be graceful, loving, and kind. Pr36

Anoint me to have a pure heart and mind forever. Pr37

Empower me to never be easily angered by criticism and accusation and to avoid quarreling about people's mistreatment of me. Pr38

Cause all the governmental leaders to praise you and come to salvation through your beloved Son Jesus Christ. Ps147

Pour from you mighty hands fresh and holy rivers of revival on all people to bring an overflow of salvation and repentance to billions of human hearts and souls. Ps147

Increase your fear and love to shine more in me and my family and in all your servants. Ps147

Let longing for your loving presence and unfailing love spring forth in my heart. Ps147

Empower my soul to love obeying your holy Word. Ps147

Strengthen my will to be upright and wise; empower my devotion to serve you and successfully bring mighty productivity in your sight. Ps147

Inspire me to praise you better with thanksgiving for the many blessings you send me. Ps147

In the name of the Lord Jesus Christ pray you.

Prayer Set 75

Holy Father, strengthen my soul to manifest always self-control in speech and action. 2Tim14

Empower me to hate all immorality. 2Tim15

Empower me to expect the blessings you have personally pronounced from your holy mouth for my life. Ps148

Provide me the resources and wisdom to produce mighty financial harvests for your glory. De46

Empower me to use the blessings you will shed on me so I can praise you with thanksgiving in holiness. Ps148

Bless me with your wisdom and favor to bring multitudes to receive your salvation and to praise you in spirit and truth so they can grow spiritually mature. Ps148

In the name of the Lord Jesus Christ I pray.

Prayer Set 76

Holy Father, make the rejoicing in the Lord Jesus Christ extremely significant in my life. Ph7

Teach me to better rejoice in the Lord Jesus Christ. Ph8

Let me walk before you in upright humbleness to praise you day and night every day. Ps149

Teach me and inspire me to perform dances when I sing of praise and exaltation with thanksgiving. Ps149

Remind me after a long time of prayer that praise and worship to you pronounce judgment on all activities of the kingdom of darkness. Ps149

In the name of the Lord of the Lord Jesus Christ I pray you.

Prayer Set 77

Holy Father, strengthen me to obey all the precepts of the new covenant of your beloved Son, the Lord Jesus Christ. Ps25

Give me your grace to overcome any voluntary sin that has been in my life. Ps25

Let your fear remain strong in my heart always. Ps5

Deliver me from the things that cause me to rebel against you. Ps25

Give me the wisdom and strength to study the path and the things that drive me to sins so I can know how to avoid them. Ps25

Anoint me to uprightly praise you in holy living everywhere by obedience to your holy Word. Ps150

Inspire me to perfectly use my body as an instrument of praise with my voice in songs of exaltation and with my arms and feet to joyfully dance for you in your presence.

In the name of the Lord Jesus Christ I pray.

Prayer Set 78

Holy Father, let your glorious flaming sword shield me, my family, and my possessions. G1

Increase in my soul and mind an overflowing creative power to multiply immensely my financial resources and productivity for your good work. G2

Let your presence remain in me, and alienate the spirits of darkness from me. G3

Allow my posterity to walk holy before you and to have godly and virtuous spouses. G4

Establish me and my posterity to gracefully fulfill the upright destiny you plan for us. G5

Let us make positive impacts on our communities and the whole world to bring your salvation to people. G6

Protect me and my posterity, and personally teach us how to obtain your blessings in this life so we can possess all you desire for us to have. G7

Anoint me and my posterity with a special motivation to lovingly obey all your instructions and your Word. G8

In the name of the Lord Jesus Christ I pray.

Prayer Set 79

Holy Father, let your Word and all your instructions remain in my mind, and empower me to meditate on them. Teach me personally how to passionately and lovingly obey them in a smooth way. Ex1

Clothe me with your priestly garments to empower me to fulfill your good work. Ex2

Anoint me with your sacred oil to walk holy in your presence. Ex3

Let my life to be spiritually radiant to bring sinners to repentance so they can have fellowship with you. Ex4

Set my body as a tabernacle that brings praise and honor to you day and night. Ex5

Enchain the power of my sinful flesh so I can rest in the peace and joy of your presence in me. Ex6

In the name of the Lord Jesus Christ I pray.

Prayer Set 80

Holy Father, inspire me to always clothe myself in holiness and manage my hair and my body in ways that bring glory to your holy presence in me. Le1

Anoint my soul to exceedingly hate any types of sexual immorality including those in media of all types. Le2

Thank you for giving your beloved Son for me as a burnt and sin offering on the cross to save my soul and to forgive me for all my sins. Le3

Thank you for allowing my Lord Jesus Christ to be a fellowship and guilt offering so I can peacefully have fellowship with you any time and without guilt. Le4

Show me the blessings you have in store for all your faithful who apply the principles of prosperity from Holy Scripture. Le5

Instruct me how to confess my sins so I can receive healing and unlock my blessings from heaven. Le6

Anoint me to be passionately motivated to give all my tithes faithfully for life. Le7

In the name of the Lord Jesus Christ I pray.

Prayer Set 81

Holy Father, empower me to lovingly and joyfully practice your holy Word and to meditate on it day and night. De1

Give me the grace and favor to proclaim the glory of your name and praise passionately the awesomeness of your majesty. De2

Provide me with the wisdom to have a wise attitude and respectable manners in your presence. De3

Send your flaming swords to secure my territories. De4

Manifest your holy presence in me, and empower me to transform my territory into an environment of prosperity to make me ride on the height of the land. De5

Bless me prosperously so I can be fed on the best food in the land you give me. De6

Pour on me your sacred anointing to empower me to please you always and to help me to never provoke you to anger. De7

In the name of the Lord Jesus Christ I pray.

Prayer Set 82

Holy Father, give me a motivated heart and mind to love meditating on your holy Word and your instructions. De8

Increase your fear and love in my soul to show more respect and honor to you. De9

Empower me with the wisdom to worship only you in this life, and give me the wisdom to not worship the devil in ignorance. De10

Let me always wear my clothing in a manner that pleases you as you inspire me and instruct me from Holy Scripture. De11

Give me the grace and favor to be fully convicted to give my first fruit to you and my tithes for my lifetime with full commitment as you command. De12

Embolden your love and fear to abide in me. Motivate me to never pray or bow before any statue fabricated by man, which you commanded us not to do. De13

Empower me to honor wisely and lovingly my mother and father. De14

In the name of the Lord Jesus Christ I pray.

Prayer Set 83

Holy Father, bless me wherever I live and wherever I go. De15

Bless the fruit of my womb, my personal business, and my jobs. De16

Bless my productivity, the work of my hand, abundantly. De17

Bless the project you have given me to achieve for your glory. Multiply immensely my posterity. De18

Foil the attack of my enemies from the realm of darkness, and let them flee before me very far. De19

Empower me to praise you and bring your fear and love to the ends of the world as you set me righteous through faith in the Lord Jesus Christ. De20

Empower me to prioritize your love and your holy Word so I can please you always, and give me the strength and wisdom to joyfully and humbly obey you. De21

In the name of the Lord Jesus Christ I pray.

Prayer Set 84

Holy Father, give me the strength to remain godly when the wicked persecute my soul. Ps37

Empower my soul with wise speech and my mouth to express what is right. Ps37

Motivate and bless me to give generously and lend to the poor without interest. Ps37

Let me always rejoice in and worship you in the Holy Spirit and in truth. Ps37

Anoint me to keep your ordinances in my heart. Ps37

Bless me with the ability to repay everything I borrow. Ps37

Create a smooth way for me to settle my debts. Ps37

Remind me, Lord, to always acknowledge and entrust my ways to you. Ps37

Give me a godly desire not to envy the rich and successful. Ps37

Anoint me with strength and wisdom to overcome anger and bitterness for life. Ps37

In the name of my Lord Jesus Christ I pray.

Part 8

The Lord will bless his people with peace (Psalm 29:11)

Prayer Set 85

Holy Father, provide mighty respect and protection for me among those who have been preoccupied with my troubles and are bitterly critical of my vulnerabilities. Ps38

Heal me from the bruises of my soul and the offenses of others who caused my sins and vulnerabilities. Ps38

Let my eyes set on you always because of your unfailing love. Ps38

Give me strength to please you. Ps38

Take away the shame in my heart that brings me grief. Ps38

Let me wait patiently for your answer. Ps38

Do not let those who insult me be above me in my time of need. Ps38

Deliver me from my enemies and sorrows. Ps38

Let me know that you are close to me to show mercy, and answer me speedily. Ps38

Heal me from all known and unknown diseases within my physical body.

In the name of the Lord Jesus Christ I pray.

Prayer Set 86

Holy Father, empower me to control myself and my mouth among evil people. Ps39

Let me fulfill gloriously and with passion and joy your work every day to the fullest extent. Ps39

Remind me every day of how short my life on earth is, and teach me to accomplish my destiny for your glory. Ps39

Give me the grace not to be ridiculed by ungodly and haughty people. Ps39

Let your compassionate and loving eyes be upon me when I call on you. Ps39

Increase the power of my strength when I am doing your work. Ps39

In the name of the Lord Jesus Christ I pray.

Prayer Set 87

Holy Father, give me the grace to declare your salvation to the ends of the world powerfully and lovingly. Ps40

Humble me to put myself at your disposal so I can joyfully go where you command me. Ps40

Empower me to reveal to people your awesome wonders and magnificent, loving plans for them. Ps40

Bring to my mind and heart new songs to praise you. Ps40

Empower me to write songs so I can worship you in private and in public. Ps40

Give me the patience to wait for your deliverance. Ps40

Deliver me from the disgrace and the deceit of the powers of darkness trying to destroy me. Ps40

Let their wicked schemes and their arrows fall short. Ps40

Anoint me to allow my eyes to always be on you in good and bad times. Ps40

In the name of the Lord Jesus Christ I pray.

Prayer Set 88

Holy Father, give me a tender heart to love and help vulnerable people. Ps41

Teach me to joyfully reserve a portion of my finances to help the poor and the fatherless infants who need help. Ps41

Provide me the resources and wisdom I need to produce a mighty financial harvest for your glory. De46

Let me be aware of you in my soul, and teach me how to please your Holy Spirit in me. Ps41

Give me the strength to seek you when the light of the Holy Spirit decreases in my soul, and allow the light of the Holy Spirit to shine brightly always in my life. Ps41

Make me stronger than my enemies. Let them see the best of me in prosperity and in uprightness. Ps41

Do not let my failures to be manifested in sight of my enemies and accusers. Ps41

Increase my trust in you and my dependency on your unfailing love and mercy. Ps41

Cause my life to be full of days with strength and excellent health. Ps41

In the name of my Lord Jesus Christ I pray.

Prayer Set 89

Holy Father, anoint and empower me to boldly love you every day. Ps42

Let the joy of my Lord Jesus Christ overwhelm my soul, and teach me to depend on it more every day. Ps42

Increase the peace of the Holy Spirit more every day in me. Ps42

Give me a strong desire to long for you every day as my only source of deliverance, comfort, satisfaction, and security. Ps42

Remind me every day to boldly expect your promises. Ps42

Rekindle my hope in you as an unending flame. Ps42

Receive favorably my petitions, thanks, and prayers for my personal needs and for the salvation of your people when I praise you. Ps42

May your unfailing love and awesome favor never depart from my life. Ps42

In the name of my Lord Jesus Christ I pray.

Prayer Set 90

Holy Father, cause my heart to have hope again when everything looks impossible and the door of deliverance seems closed. Ps43

Do not expose my shame and troubles to my adversaries, who never stop slandering and cursing my life. Ps43

Secure me under your protecting wings, and allow your riches from heaven to be showered on my life. Ps43

Fill my heart and mind with songs of praise and thanksgiving to you. Ps43

Satisfy my soul with your joy, love, and peace. Ps43

Comfort me and inspire me that you are bigger than all the troubles of my soul. Ps43

In the name of my Lord Jesus Christ I pray.

Prayer Set 91

Holy Father, bring to my memory often the awesome wonders you perform for those who walk faithfully before you. Ps44

Isolate my foes from the prosperous plan you prepare for me and from the day of my deliverance. Ps44

Restore to me everything my adversaries have plundered from my ancestors and me. Ps44

Open the door of respect for me before those who ridicule and slander my soul. Ps44

Free my life from the chain of shame. Ps44

Take me out of the pit of financial poverty. Ps44

Let my adversaries be appalled and in awe of the outpouring financial harvest and your awesome day of restoration that you have sovereignly set for my life. Ps44

Rescue me, and put me high above my enemies. Ps44

In the name of my Lord Jesus Christ I pray.

Prayer Set 92

Holy Father, empower me to honor your Word. Ps45

Let my soul be a gift of praise to you. Ps45

Anoint my heart to hate deeply all manner of wickedness. Ps45

Increase in me the wisdom to live a holy life with integrity and humility. Ps45

Manifest the culture of your holy kingdom on my life. Ps45

Give me the grace and favor to preach the gospel of your kingdom to the ends of the earth. Ps45

Cause me to always use the sword of the Holy Spirit to defend myself and your people from the power of darkness. Ps45

Increase my strength to bless you every day. Ps45

Consecrate me to bring powerful individuals to salvation and to perfectly disciple them for your glory. Ps45

Embellish richly my spiritual and natural gifts to make disciples for the Great Commission. Ps45

Empower me and bless me to represent you on earth honorably and to show your wonders, love, and mercy so people can come to salvation and worship you in spirit and in truth. Ps45

In the name of my Lord Jesus Christ I pray.

Prayer Set 93

Holy Father, anoint my heart and mind to be always fearful of you. Ps46

Remind me often to call and look to you for deliverance and take refuge in you when everything goes wrong. Ps46

Let the river that comes from your throne flow in me to rejoice my heart, to strengthen my soul, and to help me live uprightly. Ps46

Allow your presence in me to bring comfort to my soul and be the insurance that I will be victorious over my enemies. Ps46

Stop the offenses and the destructive power of my adversaries everywhere. Ps46

Destroy the arrows of the kingdom of darkness by the power of your right and your right hand. Ps46

Remind me often that you are my God, the Almighty. Ps46

Give me the grace to joyfully praise you. Ps46

In the name of the Lord Jesus Christ I pray.

Prayer Set 94

Holy Father, give me the favor and the grace to bring people of every nation to praise you in spirit and in truth. Ps47

Anoint me to magnify the glory of your kingdom to the ends of the earth. Ps47

Empower me to always testify how you delivered me from the kingdom of darkness into your glorious light by your beloved Son Jesus Christ. Ps47

Train me to declare the hope of those who believe in you and the eternal blessings you have reserved for your obedient children. Ps47

Let my body be and instrument of praise to you through the practicing of your holy Word, prayer, and songs of praise. Ps47

In the name of the Lord Jesus Christ I pray.

Prayer Set 95

Holy Father, provide me outstanding insight to visualize your awesome holiness in your throne and the ability to express it. Ps48

Manifest the majesty of your beauty on your throne and the magnificent sovereignty of your power through my life. Ps48

Let the enemies from the kingdom of darkness see your bright and shining light in me when they try to destroy me, and let the spirits of darkness flee before me at the sight of your powerfully bright and shiny presence in me. Ps48

Make my life and all my resources secure under your mighty right hand. Ps48

Let me witness every day to your goodness and power of deliverance as you did in your holy people in the past. Ps48

Anoint me to meditate of your goodness to me and to your holy nation, Israel, so I can testify of it to the ends of the earth. Ps48

Strengthen me with your joyfulness to bring those being destroyed by wickedness to repentance and salvation in the Lord Jesus Christ. Ps48

Let me witness the destruction of wickedness, hatred, and selfishness on the people of my nation. Ps48

Motivate me to count your big and small blessings and miracles in my life and those of other people. Ps48

Anoint me with the power to bring to you songs of praise and thanksgiving every day. Ps48

In the name of the Lord Jesus Christ I pray.

Prayer Set 96

Holy Father, make the rejoicing in the Lord Jesus Christ significant in my life. Ph7

Teach me to better rejoice in the Lord Jesus Christ. Ph8

Give me the grace and the power to be gentle in speech toward everyone. Ph9

Give me permanently a bold consciousness and a full awareness that you together with your beloved Son and the Holy Spirit are always in me. Ph10

Empower me to transform my anxiousness into moments of bringing you my prayers, petitions, and thanksgiving and to rejoice in you through songs of praise. Ph11

Help me bring unity to my family, your holy people, and those of this world through the gifts you have given. Ps133

Send your prosperous blessings over me and my posterity for the world to witness your glory and riches from the work you have given us to do. Ps133

In the name of the Lord Jesus Christ I pray.

Part 9

Rejoice in the Lord always; again I will say, rejoice! (Philippians 4:4)

Prayer Set 97

Holy Father, empower me with excellent devotion and great insight to study your Word so I can be always ready to present it every time I have an opportunity. Col1

Give me prudence and wisdom to determine whether or not I am in good standing in the faith especially in spiritual areas that need improvement. Col2

Give me the humility to honor and appreciate greatness from others who have done remarkable works for your glory and conducted themselves in a manner worthy of your gospel. Col3

Empower me to have excellent discipline to do well the good work you give me to do and to faithfully obey my Lord Jesus Christ. Col4

Reveal me everything in this world that is contrary to your holy Word that society regards as morally acceptable. Col5

Teach me all the holy postures and virtuous manners that reflect how people in your kingdom behave and praise you. Ps134

Teach me personally how to use financial wealth wisely and in a way that pleases you always and to bring honor and respect for your holy kingdom. Ps134

In the name of the Lord Jesus Christ I pray.

Prayer Set 98

Holy Father, give me the grace and favor to manage my anger, to never slander anyone, to speak uprightly, to avoid everything that can lead me to rage, and to wipe away every hidden malice in my life. Col8

Clothe me with humility, kindness, gentleness, compassion, and love. Col9

Empower me to receive your daily spiritual nourishment through songs of praise and exaltation from the psalms and hymnal book and then to pray with thanksgiving. Col10

Inspire me to serve you fully with all my heart, and reveal to me how you love me. Ps135

Enlighten my mind to know the wisdom behind the practice of praising and exalting you. Ps135

Bring back to me all the blessings that were stolen from me from the kingdom of darkness, and deliver my soul from their wicked chains. Ps135

Deliver me from the bad habit of unwise spending.

Increase your fear and love in my heart and mind. Ps135

In the name of the Lord Jesus Christ I pray.

Prayer Set 99

Holy Father, increase fear of you in me so I do not touch or taste anything that is contrary to your Word. Never let me entertain myself with anything that does not bring glory to you. Col6

Empower me to put to death any desires, thinking, and activities that exalt and magnify my sinful flesh such as sexual immorality, impure thoughts, lust, and evil desire. Col7

Magnify your unfailing love in my life and the security it gives to my soul. Ps136

Give me the wisdom and power to pray to you more, and inspire me to ask you the right things so I can be always a godly Christian who brings honor to you. Ps136

Empower me to make good and godly decisions so I can walk faithfully before you always. Ps136

Motivate me to read the Bible every day with full attention and to practice everything you instruct me to do from it. Ps136

Give me the power and favor to do the work you have called me to do without struggling. Ps136

In the name of the Lord Jesus Christ I pray.

Prayer Set 100

Holy Father, teach me to never embitter any one, to love everyone, and to submit to all your holy instructions. Col11

Train me to always be prudent and to pray often with thanksgiving. Col12

Give me great insight to wisely and prudently act among unbelievers so I can keep my ways in holiness. Col13

Motivate me to make the most of opportunity of your perfect gifts, your grace, and your blessings that you freely give to me. Col14

Empower me to enable my speech to be full of grace and season with salt. Col15

Give me the courage to wrestle successfully in prayer for my family and other people you inspire me to pray for. Col16

Motivate me to never rejoice in any ungodly activities in this world that society considers normal. Ps137

Instruct me in all practices in my culture that you deem immoral so I can isolate myself from them. Ps137

Pour your salve on my eyes so I can differentiate between your light and the fake light of the power of darkness so I can better live a life of sanctification. Ps137

In the name of the Lord Jesus Christ I pray.

Prayer Set 101

Holy Father, teach me all the dangers of having hairstyles the Bible says are inappropriate for your holy people. 1Tim4, De52

Teach me through scripture to know and obey the position that man and woman should fulfill in the five main ministries in your church. 1Tim5

Teach me your Word so I can please you and remain on your holy path. Ps138

Lead me to make your salvation, glory, and holiness known to multitudes. Ps138

Anoint me to walk humbly under your mighty hand every day. Ps138

Deliver me from the wicked plan of all my foes, keep me from the dominance of the kingdom of darkness, and let the work of my hand prosper mightily under your guidance. Ps138

Give me the self-motivation to praise you every day in spirit and truth. Ps138

In the name of the Lord Jesus Christ I pray.

Prayer Set 102

Holy Father, give me the resources and wisdom to produce mighty financial harvests for your glory. De46

Keep me in permanent awareness of your protective and loving eyes. Ps139

Thank you for awesomely creating me for your glory and dwelling in me to shed on my soul your salvation, happiness, peace, and love. Ps139

Thank you for planning the provision for me to be saved and to live forever with you. Ps139

Thank you also for your deep interest in my life to record in your book all my life before it happens. Ps139

Anoint my heart to hate strongly all evil activities in this world. Ps139

Empower me to better my ways before you in holiness. Ps139

In the name of the Lord Jesus Christ I pray.

Prayer Set 103

Holy Father, vanquish the agenda of the kingdom of darkness against my life. Enchain daily all their weapons destined to bring shame and trouble to my life. Ps140

Make a quick and easy way for me to be out of the trap of wickedness. Ps140

Do not allow plunderers and immoral individuals to fulfill any high governmental position of leadership in my country. Ps140

Bring a multitude of godly and moral individuals to all governmental positions in strong agreement with your biblical instruction. Ps140

Let moral individuals who live in perfect agreement with your Holy Scripture win elections and secure justice for their constituents. Ps140

In the name of the Lord Jesus Christ I pray.

Prayer Set 104

Holy Father, empower me to always pursue what is right and godly according to your faithful Word. 1Tim6

Let your love in me to be practical toward every one as you freely provide it to me. Anoint me to always pursue righteousness, godliness, faith, love, patience, and gentleness more than financial riches. 1Tim7

Remind me to remain boldly content in you in times of great distress by magnifying your holy presence in me by songs of exaltation and praise and through prayer and petitions with thanksgiving to you. 2Tim18

Anoint my speech and my thought to be godly so I can please you all the time. Ps141

Let the desire of my soul be holy, and empower me to cast away impure desires. Ps141

Empower me with humility to receive instruction and disciplinary correction from your accomplished holy leaders you put above me to help me mature spiritually. Ps141

Protect me from the daily oppressive attack of the realm of darkness, and enlighten my eyes to see their wickedness so I can escape their traps. Ps141

In the name of the Lord Jesus Christ I pray.

Prayer Set 105

Holy Father, give me the favor and grace to love you more than myself and to use money as a tool to please you and to be at your service. 2Tim5

Teach me and empower me how to not be boastful in anything. 2Tim6

Anoint me to be courageous and bold in rejecting wicked thoughts and desires. 2Tim3

Inspire me with zero tolerance for imprudence and to avoid foolish and stupid arguments and quarrels. 2Tim4

Give me the favor and grace to fulfill the honorable destiny you have for me. Ps142

Empower me to avoid making unreasonable arguments. Ps142

Give me the grace to convince others lovingly and with respect to receive the Lord Jesus Christ. Ps142

In the name of the Lord Jesus Christ I pray.

Prayer Set 106

Holy Father, give me the grace not to be too proud of myself and not be wise in my own eyes. 2Tim7

Teach me to treat myself better and not make decisions that will harm my life. 8

Deliver me from all the troubles that have been too long in my life. Increase my patience to wait expectantly on you joyfully for your promises to me. Ps143

Empower me and my family to use the internet for your glory. Ps143

Give me the favor to overcome the distresses and sorrows of life. Ps143

Provide me the wisdom and the strength to be like Jesus. Ps143

Give me the grace and favor for mighty, innovative, and creative power for excellence and for mighty financial harvest and productivity to better support your good work in the world. Ps143

In the name of the Lord Jesus Christ I pray.

Prayer Set 107

Holy Father, thank you for teaching me to receive your heavenly blessings and your wisdom to live a holy life. Ps144

Let the Holy Spirit remain in my soul, and permit your loving-kindness and unfailing love to rekindle my hope. Ps144

Increase my expectation of the promises that come through the death and resurrection of the Lord Jesus Christ. Ps144

Remind me to rely only on you instead of human beings. Ps144

Take the enemies from the invisible realm out of my territory, and protect it with your shield from all the power and weapons of the enemy. Ps144

Rekindle the power of prudence in my life so I can stay away from every trap of the devil kingdom in this world. Ps144

Strengthen my commitment for tithing and for helping vulnerable individuals such as fatherless children everywhere. Ps144

Empower me to worship you better and more often in spirit and in truth. Ps144

Strike with your great, sharp, fierce, fiery, double-edged sword my enemies in the realm of darkness that come to trouble my life and steal my blessings. Ps144

Blossom and embellish my intelligence, land, and social manners to reveal the glory of your holy kingdom.

Isolate my enemies from my territories and path. Ps144

Thank you for being my fortress, salvation, happiness, security, and peace. Ps144

In the name of the Lord Jesus Christ I pray.

Prayer Set 108

Holy Father, let me always trust in you and abide humbly in your Word with a bold hope of my salvation. Ps49

Show me the teaching of the grace that provides true salvation in your kingdom. Ps49

Empower me to never put my trust in material possessions. Ps49

Teach me to praise you with my possessions and especially when they are in abundance. Ps49

Motivate me with your wisdom to manage my possessions and store my treasure in heaven. Ps49

Anoint me boldly in my heart to never love or put my hope in earthly riches. Ps49

Empower me to never seek the praise of people. Ps49

Inspire me how to always humble myself in any state of life. Ps49

Cause me to understand well the teaching of the gospel of salvation by grace that will truly prepare my way to heaven. Ps49

Increase your wisdom in me so I can declare the truthfulness of your Word and demonstrate its majesty and power. Ps49

In the name of the Lord Jesus Christ I pray.

Part 10

There is a river whose streams make glad the city of God. (Psalm 46:4)

Prayer Set 109

Holy Father, let me boldly and truly abide in your grace, which ensures my way to your heavenly kingdom. Ps50

Enlighten my mind and eyes so I can see your just eternal judgment on those who choose to live proudly in wickedness. Ps50

Empower me to faithfully obey you and practice your holy words. Ps50

Train me to obey the instructions and commands of the Lord Jesus Christ through the Holy Spirit. Ps50

Anoint me to love all your precepts and passionately exalt your holy Word. Ps50

Empower me with a special gift of devotion to speak wisely on your behalf and to enjoy doing things that please you. Ps50

Give me the strength to gladly serve you, follow your commands, and obey your precepts. Ps50

Train me to never befriend wicked people and never participate in their ungodliness. Ps50

Anoint my heart to sincerely love others and show them compassion in their suffering. Ps50

In the name of the Lord Jesus Christ I pray.

Prayer Set 110

Holy Father, provide me with your grace to overcome my weakness and wrongdoing. Ps51

Empower me to overcome my improper vulnerabilities. Ps51

Manifest the joy of the Lord Jesus Christ in my heart, let me be fully aware of it, and help me rely on this joy above others. Ps51

Increase the presence of the Holy Spirit in me, and allow your love to guide my heart. Ps51

Increase the peace of the Holy Spirit in my life to embolden the security of my soul in this spiritually persecuted world. Ps51

Empower me to exalt the blood of the Lord Jesus Christ that wipes away my iniquity. Ps51

Magnify your fear in me so I can embrace with all my heart the gift of salvation and can humbly please you in holiness through my actions. Ps51

Let my life be a holy example for others so hope can remain in the hearts of the vulnerable. Ps51

Give me the strength and wisdom to learn and understand your holy Word so I can obey you in truth. Ps51

Sustain me by your Holy Spirit so I can please you. Ps51

In the name of the Lord Jesus Christ I pray.

Prayer Set 111

Holy Father, empower my heart to never rejoice in anything that does not bring glory to you, and train my mouth to exalt you at all times. Ps52

Bless me to be a mighty builder for the work of the Great Commission to increase citizen in your holy kingdom. Ps52

Teach me to use part of my financial resources to help vulnerable people, especially orphans.

Give me the character to always tell the truth. Ps52

Bless and motivate me to support the poor and help those who live in poverty. Ps52

Train me to put my confidence in you alone, not in earthly riches, and provide me the power to strengthen the faith of others. Ps52

Give me the confidence to always rely on you when I am enduring unbearable problems. Ps52

Let your compassion and your merciful grace never depart from me. Ps51

In the name of the Lord Jesus Christ I pray.

Prayer Set 112

Holy Father, empower me with a strong devotion to praise you daily through worship, song, and prayer. Ps53

Cause my life to be holy through all my conduct. Ps53

Give me the grace and the power of leadership to successfully accomplish the work you have called me to do.

Anoint my soul to seek you always for guidance and to pray for peace. Ps53

Strengthen and train me to search for you often through prayer for the salvation of all unsaved people. Ps53

Let me be always joyfully confident in you and full of hope and expectation of your promises in this world saturated with troubles. Ps53

Raise my head high with respect and honor above the ungodly. Ps53

Thank you for the salvation of my soul that you provided me in your beloved Son Jesus Christ. Ps53

In the name of the Lord Jesus Christ I pray.

Prayer Set 113

Holy Father, let your shield protect me from the evil arrows of the kingdom of darkness. Ps54

Pour in my spirit a fresh anointing of prudence and godliness, and increase your faith in me to bring down all the stronghold of evilness. Ps54

Deliver me from all evil traps. Ps54

Vanquish the wicked plans of all my enemies. Ps54

Deliver me from those working for the destruction of my life and family. Ps54

Anoint me to sing new songs of praise and thanksgiving often to you. Ps54

Exalt me above my enemies in spiritual victory and financial prosperity. Ps54

In the name of the Lord Jesus Christ I pray.

Prayer Set 114

Holy Father, deliver me from the abusive power of darkness. Ps55

Provide strength and healing to my soul to overcome the scary tactics of the kingdom of wickedness, lifelessness, and senseless. Ps55

Let me take refuge in you first when my adversaries declare war against me. Ps55

Allow a mighty increase of your joy, love, and peace in my life so I can courageously face the horrible activities of the powers of darkness. Ps55

Hand me the keys to triumph over my enemies. Ps55

Bring down the destructive plans of my foes to plunder my resources and destroy me and my family. Ps55

Empower me to worship you in peace and security. Ps55

Provide me the resources and wisdom to produce mighty financial harvests for your glory. De46

In the name of the Lord Jesus Christ I pray.

Prayer Set 115

Holy Father, protect me from the snares of the kingdom of darkness. Ps56

Strengthen my heart when spirits of wickedness are depressing my soul. Ps56

Come down to me with your mighty army for my defense.

Deliver me from the attack of the power of darkness. Ps56

Enchain every demon and spirit of darkness that pursues me. Ps56

Let all the spirits of thieves and destruction flee before me in seven ways when they come to me in one way. Ps56

Wipe away my tears and sorrow when I am under wicked oppression. Ps56

Fill me with your joy, peace, and love to overcome the psychological warfare of my foes. Ps56

Empower me to pray often and bring songs of praise and prayers of thanksgiving to you. Ps56

In the name of the Lord Jesus Christ I pray.

Prayer Set 116

Holy Father, allow me to be aware of your merciful power of deliverance through my life when the enemy depresses my soul. Ps57

Let me witness your overcoming power of contentment in my life when the solution to my problems is not there yet. Ps57

Permit hope to remain in my soul when I cry out to you. Ps57

Do not let the enemy put me to shame from their slander and plans to destroy me. Ps57

Deliver me from the ambush that the kingdom of darkness set to destroy me. Ps57

Defend me from those too powerful for me. Ps57

Deliver me from the powers that block me from exploring my resources and abilities. Ps57

Destroy the plan, the agenda, and the mind-set of those who have greater power than I do and are working to keep me poor and dependent on them. Ps57

Send qualified people my way to help me explore all my resources and abilities. Ps57

Help me rescue my unexplored abilities and resources you have deposit in my soul and in this world. Ps57

Train me to use all my resources and abilities to praise, honor, and please you. Ps57

In the name of the Lord Jesus Christ I pray.

Prayer Set 117

Holy Father, manifest a passionate, godly love in my soul for everybody no matter their color, nationality, or faith. 2Jo1

Teach me to passionately obey all your instructions. 2

Give me the prudence and your fear to never deviate from the teaching of my Lord Jesus Christ. 2Jo3

Empower me to manage excellently all my responsibilities in my family as instructed in scripture. Ps58

Protect me from the slanders of evil people who work tirelessly to destroy me. Ps58

Wipe away corruption and injustice from all institutions in my country. Ps58

Bring your mighty judgment on corruption and injustice in all institutions in my country. Ps58

Let me rejoice in praising you through songs and prayers of thanksgiving when corruption and injustice are banished from our society. Ps58

Cause the world to see that it is you who brings prosperity to our country so everyone can seek and fear you. Ps58

In the name of the Lord Jesus Christ I pray.

Prayer Set 118

Holy Father, show no mercy to corrupt institutions that cause vulnerable people to be abused, plundered, exploited, and impoverished. Ps59

Turn unjust agendas into policies that help vulnerable people and countries to come out of poverty and social insecurity. Ps59

Bring godly global leaders to power to summon the unjust and abusive institutions in the world to justice.

Cause laws to be enacted globally and nationally to set zero tolerance policies regarding corruption and injustice. Ps59

Empower governmental leaders to increase and embolden national and global infrastructures so billions of people can come out of abject poverty. Ps59

Enlighten the minds and hearts of world leaders to sincerely and always seek peace with one other. Ps59

Cause the world leaders also to make good decision to increase investments for new and secure jobs to lessen the burdens of vulnerable citizens. Ps59

In the name of the Lord Jesus Christ I pray.

Prayer Set 119

Holy Father, thank you for delivering us from your wrath, forgiving our wrongdoings, and having mercy on us. Ps60

Change our distress and shame to joy, peace, and confidence in you. Ps60

Let us pray to you in unity of hearts and faith, and help us remain faithful to you. Ps60

Encourage us to bring praise and reverence to your holy name. Ps60

Let our hope in you remain strong, and strengthen us to expect your blessings. Ps60

Help us destroy all man-made idols, and rain a spiritual revival continually on the world. Ps60

Cause us to worship you always in spirit and in truth and never to bow before statues so we can bring glory only to you. Ps60

Deliver us from our persecutors and foes who are stronger than we are. Ps60

Make us stronger than our enemies, and equip us to always subdue our foes. Ps60

Let your virtuous success abide in us as a strong belt around our waists. Ps60

In the name of the Lord Jesus Christ I pray.

Prayer Set 120

Holy Father, empower me with your grace and favor and a bold humility to joyfully be a slave of righteousness in complete obedience and passionate devotion to you. Ro7

Teach me to be a slave of righteousness. Ro8

Give me the favor, grace, and strength to be a slave of righteousness so I can live in perfect holiness through all my conduct. Ro9

Motivate me to be gladly your slave forever. Ro10

Let me productively use the gift of eternal life for your glory. Ro11

Empower me to prioritize your beloved Son as my Savior who wipes away my sins as well as my Lord, whom I must obey forever. Ro12

Grant me success and protection in this world from all the entrapments of the kingdom of darkness. Ps121

Embolden my expectation of all your blessed promises to me. Let my praise to you be acceptable every day. Ps121

In the name of the Lord Jesus Christ I pray.

Part 11

Is anyone among you in trouble? Let them pray. (James 5:13 NKJV)

Prayer Set 121

Holy Father, inspire me through your Holy Spirit to follow the teaching of the Lord Jesus Christ and the instructions of his holy apostles in scripture. Ro13

Teach me to be led by you and fully controlled by the Holy Spirit to perfectly work at your service in holiness and productivity with great success and in a manner that pleases you. Ro14

Empower me to watch, control, and overcome the sinful power of my flesh and to walk in submission and guidance of the Holy Spirit. Ro15

Give me the favor to have a perfect relationship with you for life. Ps122

Cause my relationship with you to be mightily productive and praiseworthy to you. Ps122

Strengthen and inspire me to pray for spiritual revival and peace on earth. Ps122

May the blessings of abundant spiritual and financial prosperity spring forth in my life forever for your glory and good work. Ps122

In the name of the Lord Jesus Christ I pray.

Prayer Set 122

Holy Father, motivate me to accept and endure the suffering that comes from living a godly life. Ro16

Thank you for the Holy Spirit of life you send to advocate for me and help me overcome my weaknesses. Ro17

Show me how to keep your peace and joy in me when troubles, sorrows, and illness sadden my soul. Ro18

Give me the endurance to use my body as a holy sacrifice that pleases you. Ro19

Reveal to me social activities that are regarded as morally right in this world but are opposed to your holy Word, and give me the grace to isolate myself from them. 20

Give me a bold patience and a strong expectation to wait for your awesome blessings and favor. Ps123

Let your joy and peace overflow my soul like a mighty stream. Ps123

Increase my hope and trust in you every day. Ps123

In the name of the Lord Jesus Christ I pray.

Prayer Set 123

Holy Father, teach me to always honor high governmental authorities.

Empower my speech to avoid criticism of spiritual and governmental leaders, and empower me to spend time in prayer for them so they can successfully overcome the challenges they face. 21

Bless me to always pay my taxes, and let me always obey the law. Ro22

Empower me to use my body as your temple in ways that please and satisfy the Holy Spirit, who dwells in my soul.

Reveal clearly through scripture the godly ways men and women should dress, treat their hair, and manage their manners in church. 1Tim4, De52

Teach me according to the Bible what types of positions and activities that men and women can fulfill and do through the five main ministries that scripture reveals.

Let me be aware of your presence in me when distress besets my soul. Ps124

Strengthen me, and deliver me from the peril of life. Ps124

Anoint me to bring your praise and honor to the ends of the world because of your worthiness. Ps124

In the name of the Lord Jesus Christ I pray.

Prayer Set 124

Holy Father, show me how not to receive your grace in vain. 2Co1

Empower me with your favor to use your grace in a godly way. 2

Embolden my commitment and strength to follow in holiness and in humbleness the Lord Jesus Christ every day. 3

Cause me to know with your insight the grace that gives eternal life according to your holy Word so I can rely on the Lord Jesus Christ's instructions with true hope of salvation. Ga1

Enlighten my understanding and my eyes to walk according to the Holy Spirit from his holy guidance. Ga2

Give me a bold fear of you and the power to prioritize the desire of the Holy Spirit in my heart above all my personal needs and desires. Ga3

Rain your favor over me, and protect me all around with your shield. Ps125

Embolden my trust in you for any trivial circumstances of life. Ps125

Deliver me from my persecutors, and let them clearly acknowledge your glory and love in me to attract them to repentance and salvation. Ps125

In the name of the Lord Jesus Christ I pray.

Prayer Set 125

Holy Father, empower me to overcome the ungodly desires of my sinful nature. Ga4

Show me how to nullify the power of my sinful nature in my thinking, desires, and actions. Ga5

Teach me to mightily produce the fruit of the Holy Spirit through everything in my life. Ga6

Empower me to joyfully help others carry their burdens without grumbling or complaint. Ga7

Give me the grace to sow the seed of the Holy Spirit in my heart and destroy every seed of the flesh sown in my soul. Ga8

Restore all the blessings the stealers in the realm of darkness have taken from me. Ps126

Let me securely receive my financial mighty harvest from the multitude of financial seeds I have sown in your good soil. Ps126

Inspire in me new songs of thanksgiving and praise to exalt you every day. Ps126

In the name of the Lord Jesus Christ I pray.

Prayer Set 126

Holy Father, bless my soul to be an excellent environment, fertile soil for your holy Word to take deep root in. Ep1

Empower me to sow financial and spiritual seeds in fertile ground so I can reap always in every season a mighty harvest of financial and spiritual wealth. Ep2

Give me the grace to always be humble through everything I do. Ep3

Build my life as you desire, and empower me to fulfill my blessed destiny and the godly, outstanding vision you have in mind for me. Ps127

Cause me and my posterity to be always obedient to you, to practice all your precepts, and to possess our land, territory, and resources without debt. Ps127

Multiply greatly my posterity to serve you in holiness and to bring praise to you. Ps127

Give me and all my posterity the grace to overcome our sinful nature and every wicked entrapment of the realm of darkness to secure our salvation in your mighty hand. Ps127

In the name of the Lord Jesus Christ I pray.

Prayer Set 127

Holy Father, anoint my head and heart to keep the fear and love of you in me to remain always strong. Ps128

Empower me to practice your Word with exceeding joy and comfort. Ps128

Give my spouse the favor and grace to be delivered from all past persecutions. Ps128

Empower my spouse to bring prosperously mighty fruits of righteousness. Ps128

Instruct personally my loved ones how to please you and keep your fear and love ablaze in their lives. Ps128

Allow me to see my descendants to the third generation, so I can personally bless them and pray with them. Ps128

Provide me the right resources and wisdom to produce mighty financial harvest for your glory. De46

In the name of the Lord Jesus Christ I pray.

Prayer Set 128

Holy Father, give me a bold patience and love to joyfully support others who are slow learners and spiritually weak. Ep4

Teach me to produce godly fruits in my family and among your people in helping them keep unity and peace in themselves and with the Holy Spirit. Ep5

Train me to never give the kingdom of darkness any inch in my life, especially through anger, lies, slander, rage, or bitterness. Ep6

Protect my life from the abusive cursing of my slanderers, surround my blessings with your inaccessible shield to nullify the power of the plunderers, and bring back seven times everything that they have stolen from me. Ps129

Bless my hands to be excellent stewards regarding financial blessings, shield my hands to waste no money, and empower them to manage productively well all my resources. Ps129

Break in pieces the chain that handicaps my abilities for success, and vanquish all the curses that inflict tribulation in my life. Ps129

Eliminate my enemies' destructive weapons and agenda they use to shame and harm me life. Ps129

In the name of the Lord Jesus Christ I pray.

Prayer Set 129

Holy Father, empower me to never grieve the Holy Spirit in my life. Ep7

Give me the grace and favor to totally have the power to overcome angriness, bitterness, lying, and slander. Ep8

Teach me to successfully have zero tolerance for sexual immorality, greed, and all impure thoughts and desires. Ep9

Thank you for providing forgiveness for my sins through the blood of your beloved Son Jesus Christ. Ps130

Thank you also for taking my soul out of death and away from the path of hell. Ps130

Embolden my expectation of your promises patiently, and keep alive wisely the vision you bestow in my heart so it can be accomplished. Ps130

Teach me and my posterity how not to take for granted all the blessings that come from the grace of your salvation. Ps130

In the name of the Lord Jesus Christ I pray. Ps130

Prayer Set 130

Holy Father, give me grace and favor to live in a manner worthy and honorable of the gospel of Christ. Ph1

Empower me to continue to work out my salvation with fear, obedience, and humility by the guidance of the Holy Spirit in me. Ph2

Manifest your purpose and my destiny in my life through the gifts you give me to do your good work. Ph3

Train me to hold firm joyfully to the Word of life without complaint. Ph4

Humble me to be inspired by your exemplary and blameless holy people and to imitate their good way of serving you. Ph5

Motivate me to stand firm in the Lord Jesus Christ. Ph6

Give me the grace and favor to be humble in everything in this life. Ps131

Let me be fully aware of your joy that come with the anointing of the Holy Spirit in my heart, and motivate me to give you thanks in my prayer for this mighty blessing. Ps131

Increase my trust in you and my expectation every day for everything you are helping me achieve for your glory. Ps131

In the name of the Lord Jesus Christ I pray.

Prayer Set 131

Holy Father, thank you for making my body your holy temple to personally reside in me. Ps132

Thank you for allowing your beloved Son to suffer on the cross for my sin, which allowed me to become your child so I can live with you forever. Ps132

Give me the power to wisely and boldly proclaim your love and salvation everywhere in gratitude for your outstanding grace and favor in the Lord Jesus Christ. Ps132

Change my financial resources of just enough to a flow of abundance, more than just enough. Ps132

Vanquish the plan of the enemies to block and destroy my power of creativity and productivity for financial prosperity and your good work that you entrusted to me. Ps132

Allow me and my posterity to overcome the path of iniquity and negligence toward your holy Word. Ps132

Empower me to bring multitudes to repentance and receive your salvation. Ps132

Increase in my soul the joy of the Lord Jesus Christ, the peace of the Holy Spirit, and your love every day. Ps132

In the name of the Lord Jesus Christ I pray.

Prayer Set 132

Holy Father, let me fulfill successfully the vision you manifest in my heart to accomplish. Ps61

Provide me your favor and grace to accomplish every promise you have pronounced over my life. Ps61

Let my life be full of excellent health to bring more people into your kingdom. Ps61

Set my heart to rejoice in you always. Ps61

Give me the wisdom and blessings to abundantly increase my treasures in your kingdom. Ps61

Anoint my soul to enjoy praising you more and forever in songs and prayer. Ps61

Secure my life under the power of your mighty hand from the terror of my foes. Ps61

In the name of the Lord Jesus Christ I pray.

Part 12

Is anyone among you in trouble? Let them pray. (James 5:13 NKJV)

Prayer Set 133

Holy Father, comfort me always when the confusing troubles of this world come to overwhelm my soul. Ps62

Let your salvation shine in my heart as the sun lightens the sky. Ps62

Secure my life from the ambushes of my enemies. Ps62

Make me stronger than those who attack me without cause. Ps62

Teach me of your awesome power and tender mercy.

Anoint my head to have boldly your fear and your passionate love in my heart. Ps62

Provide me the resources and wisdom to produce mighty financial harvests for your glory. De46

Train me to praise you better and better every day. Ps62

Empower me to love obeying your commands all the time. Ps62

Increase mightily your love in me. Ps62

In the name of the Lord Jesus Christ I pray.

Prayer Set 134

Holy Father, bring down the arrogance of the wicked that troubles my life. Ps63

Increase my dependency on your loving presence in me to bring my soul to thirst and seek for you every day. Ps63

Let my foes acknowledge your compassion for me, and let them know your graceful power is protecting me. Ps63

Give me bold insurance of imminent victory over those who persecute me without cause. Ps63

Let me praise you while we wait for the mighty victory as I exalt you in patience and hope during times of trouble.

Allow my foes to have great fear of you when you put me above them in prosperity and success. Ps63

Cause my mouth to exalt joyfully the Lord Jesus Christ through praises and prayers of thanksgiving before all nations and in great assemblies. Ps63

In the name of the Lord Jesus Christ I pray.

Prayer Set 135

Holy Father, protect me from the curses of my slanderers, and deliver me from their ambushes. Ps64

Destroy the plot of the kingdom of darkness to plunder my blessings. Ps64

Cause all my resources and riches to be successfully explored in my life for your glory when the power of darkness opposes me. Ps64

Increase in me your favor and grace for me to explore mightily all the productive resources and gifts you give me in my country and other countries. Ps64

Vanquish the activities and agendas of my adversaries that stop me from growing in wisdom, strength, unity, brotherly kindness, and financial prosperity. Ps64

Destroy the agenda and the vision of our foes that cause distress and trouble in our families and territories. Ps64

Bring down completely the arrogance of those who are working tirelessly to destroy our lives. Ps64

Deliver our country from financial problems from the sight of all nations with the power of your right hand, and let the world be aware that it is you who is blessing us. Ps64

Let us praise you so the world witnesses your rich compassion for your people. Ps64

In the name of Lord Jesus Christ I pray.

Prayer Set 136

Holy Father, enlighten my eyes and spirit to see your goodness and merciful wonders toward humankind. Ps65

Give me the discipline and power to record the manifestation of your abundant love and your rich grace in my life and others so I can bring praise to you in great assemblies. Ps65

Thank you for all my sins you have forgiven. Ps65

Anoint my soul to have a great sense of responsibility to never take in vain the gift of salvation. Ps65

Instruct me about your loving patience so I can bring encouragement and hope to those who are weak in the faith, and help them live holy lives so they can ensure their salvation. Ps65

Empower me to proclaim the majesty of your faithfulness and your loving-kindness through the preaching of the gospel of your kingdom. Ps65

Inspire me to imitate your ways through the comfort of your loving-kindness so people can see your glory and gain salvation. Ps65

Thank you for allowing trees to produce plenty of fruits so the godly and the wicked alike can have food. Ps65

In the name of the Lord Jesus Christ I pray.

Prayer Set 137

Holy Father, anoint my heart and mind to forever hate practicing all sin. Ps66

Give me a wise and prudent attitude to isolate myself from any sinful path and anything that causes people to sin. Ps66

Teach me to avoid every path that leads me to sin. Ps66

Empower me not to admire and never to keep sin in my heart. Ps66

Give me the grace to cause multitudes to worship you in spirit and truth. Ps66

Allow my life to reveal your fearful and loving glory to inspire people to live a holy life in sanctification so they can enjoy your infinitely prosperous blessings through intimacy with you. Ps66

Mold me to be a vase of honor to attract others to you to securely have eternal life under your mighty hand. Ps66

Anoint my soul to praise you with a passionate and deep love for you in all sincerity of heart with all kind of prayers and songs of exaltation and thanksgiving. Ps66

In the name of the Lord Jesus Christ I pray.

Prayer Set 138

Holy Father, empower me to be always humble in everything and to have a contrite heart. Ps67

Motivate me to passionately apply successful all the principles of blessing and financial prosperity written in scripture, and help me live according to your precepts. Ps67

Embolden my soul to pray all kinds of faithful prayers daily to you as your holy apostles have directed us to do in the Bible. Ps67

Train me with successful discipline, strength, and wisdom to pray for peace and mighty spiritual revival in the world. Ps67

Teach me the priority my Lord Jesus Christ has commanded all his disciples to observe. Ps67

Empower me to successfully discipline all my children in a smooth way to bring them to greatly fear and love you at the same time. Ps67

Increase the fear of the Holy Spirit and his love in me so I can practice his commands. Ps67

In the name of the Lord Jesus Christ I pray.

Prayer Set 139

Holy Father, give me the courage and wisdom to declare your eternal sovereignty and your judgment on the wicked who refuse to repent and who choose to walk away from your holy Word. Ps68

Bless me more financially to manifest your loving-kindness in supporting vulnerable Christian families and others who are struggling for work, food, and shelter. Ps68

Give me the grace to attract multitudes to serve you. Ps68

Let your salvation reach every mind and heart on earth. Ps68

Train and bless me to bring your glory and salvation to multitudes. Ps68

Enlighten my spirit to attract people to receive the Lord Jesus Christ. Ps68

In the name of the Lord Jesus Christ I pray.

Prayer Set 140

Holy Father, give me a mighty gift of healing and the manifestation of your wonders to bring hope and deliverance through salvation to those who have been severely suffering due to the power of darkness. Ps69

Deliver me from all my troubles so your people can be revived and worship you in spirit and truth. Ps69

Camp around me with the power of your right and of your right hand to bring down the power of darkness that distresses my life. Ps69

Let your mighty warrior angels pursue the army of wickedness that comes to plunder my blessings and destroy my life. Ps69

Let your mighty army break their bows, destroy their arrows, and scatter those evil spirits away from me. Ps69

Manifest your joy in my soul to pray to you in peace. Ps69

Put me above my foes, and make me stronger than my enemies. Ps69

Pour your prosperous blessings on me to fulfill the Great Commission. Ps69

In the name of the Lord Jesus Christ I pray.

Prayer Set 141

Holy Father, destroy the traps of all foes who plan to destroy me and my family. Ps70

Enchain all spirits of darkness that have been bringing shame and destruction in my life in a deep pit far from me. Ps70

Deliver me from human persecutors, and give me the love and courage to deal with them kindly. Ps70

Rekindle boldly my hope in you to proclaim the goodness of your holy name and your salvation. Ps70

Rescue me from the stealers and the destroyers, and answer my prayers speedily. Ps70

In the name of the Lord Jesus Christ I pray.

Prayer Set 142

Holy Father, train me and give me your grace to be honorable, respectable, and godly and to show your power in this society to attract multitudes to holy living and salvation. Ps71

Let your glorious presence in me inspire me to write new songs of praise and thanksgiving, and give me a strong motivation to live a life of integrity. Ps71

Manifest in my heart always gratitude to you to incite me to praise and worship you always because of the provision of salvation through my Lord Jesus Christ. Ps71

Give me a continual desire to devote my life to praise and to please you through prayer and song and following your holy Word. Ps71

Empower me to bring to every living being on earth a full awareness of your sovereignty in all your creation. Ps71

Give me the grace to express through my daily life your unchangeable loving-kindness and your unfailing faithfulness. Ps71

Increase in me your wisdom, prudence, and courage to make godly decision always for your glory. Ps71

Help me overcome all the traps of the kingdom of darkness and their distresses from my soul, and answer my petitions. Ps71

Remind me daily that the deliverance of your faithful ones from their enemies is certain. Ps71

In the name of the Lord Jesus Christ I pray.

Prayer Set 143

Holy Father, help all leaders in the world establish justice in their countries. Ps72

Empower all legislators to work in unity with their executive branches to enact laws of justice and godliness in their lands and especially laws concerning religious tolerance. Ps72

Motivate all governmental institutions to enforce laws of justice and godliness. Ps72

Show your holy and sanctified church how to manifest your holy culture through their community daily as it is in your kingdom. Ps72

Cause the most powerful leaders on earth to fully and respectfully support the most vulnerable people and nations. Ps72

Manifest your salvation and a mighty spiritual revival on all people in the world. Ps72

Reach every leader in the world to know your salvation, and teach them all how to successfully fight hunger, physical abuse, sex slavery, and pornography. Ps72

Make your abundant riches available to all who need them. Ps72

Establish true worship in spirit and truth to be predominant in the world. Ps72

In the name of the Lord Jesus Christ I pray.

Prayer Set 144

Holy Father, guide me to be inspired deeply and to be affected by the exemplary lives of your faithful servants in the Bible and in this life. 2Tim19

Bless and empower me with bold courage to fulfill the duties of my heavenly calling through the perfect gifts you provide me. 2Tim21

Provide me true spiritual insight and biblical wisdom to clearly identify religious doctrinal error, human traditions, and myths that are contrary to the gospel of grace and the teaching of the Lord Jesus Christ. Ti1

Enlarge my understanding of the gospel of grace that teaches not to be ungodly. Ti2

Secure my vitality, strength, health, and spirit when the enemy keeps sending spiritual and physical diseases, sleepiness, weakness, and laziness. Ps109

Safeguard my financial harvest and wealth and my family with love when the enemy conspires to steal my finances and bring poverty and dispute into my family life. Ps109

In the name of the Lord Jesus Christ I pray.

Part 13

Devote yourselves to prayer, being watchful and thankful. (Colossians 4:2)

Prayer Set 145

Holy Father, permit your mighty door of financial prosperity and blessings to continually remain open to me, and destroy my enemies' agenda to bring wrath into my life. Ps110

Expand your blessed promises in every area of my life, and let them continue from generation to generation. Ps110

Give me the grace to have in my company qualified and gifted workers in the ministry to help me accomplish the good work you entrusted to me to do. Ps110

Send always your mighty angelic army to defend me in times of danger. Ps110

Open the stores of your heavens, and pour day and night all kind of blessing on my life to exhibit your abundant wealth on earth for your glory. De48

Seal with your royal signet ring all your blessed promises you plan for me. Ps110

Vanquish the destructive power of darkness that comes to persecute my soul. Ps110

In the name of the Lord Jesus Christ I pray.

Prayer Set 146

Holy Father, empower me to pray for all government leaders in the world as your holy apostle command in the book of Timothy. 1Tim1

Humble me to praise you in sincerity of heart, and give me the grace and favor to always properly clothe myself with decency according to your holy instructions. 1Tim2

Inspire me to honor you and please you by wearing godly clothing. 1Tim3

Let my life be a public testimony to your glory everywhere.

Let my fear and love for you never depart my heart and mind. Ps111

Give me the favor to conquer many territories for the propagation of the gospel. Ps111

Open my understanding to comprehend the instructions of the Holy Spirit for spiritual and financial success. Ps111

In the name of the Lord Jesus Christ I pray.

Prayer Set 147

Holy Father, remind me to never take vengeance on those who hurt me and to bring my sorrow to you, but deliver me from the distresses of those troublemakers. 1Thes13

Empower me to always pray with thanksgiving and rejoice always in you only. 1Thes14

Strengthen me to keep everything honorable and good and abandon all that is dishonest and harmful. 1Thes15

Manifest in my heart and mind a great respect for you when I am in your presence. Ps112

Anoint my soul to joyfully obey your holy Word with love. Ps112

Make clear to me the riches and gifts you bestow on me, and empower me to use them wisely and productively for your glory.

Bless me when others ask me for help so I can lessen their problems. Ps112

In the name of the Lord Jesus Christ I pray.

Prayer Set 148

Holy Father, increase my strength to courageously follow my Lord Jesus Christ and all his instruction through his apostles' instructions. 1Thes1

Let your love overflow in my heart for everyone. 1Thes2

Allow your holy presence in me to strengthen my heart every day. 1Thes3

Give me your grace and favor to have full control of my body. 1Thes4

Open my eyes and understanding to be fully sanctified in this wicked world. 1Thes5

Empower me with the full conviction to hate, reject, and avoid sexual immorality in all its forms and practices. 1Thes6

Wipe away the shame of my past from my soul. Ps113

Change the financial bareness in my life into mighty financial wealth to bring your praise everywhere. Ps113

In the name of the Lord Jesus Christ I pray.

Prayer Set 149

Holy Father, give me the grace to not be impulsive in speech and action and not to be disloyal to you in service and with people. 2Tim16

Empower me with the humility to never think too highly of myself in any circumstances. 2Tim17

Empower me to refute the lies of the kingdom of darkness in society. Heb1

Thank you for sending your beloved son Jesus Christ to be judged in my place on the cross for my sins.

Take me out of the bondage of poverty and spiritual ignorance, and empower me with physical and spiritual strength. Ps114

Empower me to successfully use the gifts you provide me to bring people to your holy heaven. Ps114

Vanquish the plunderers who are plotting to take away my precious resources that are reserved for your godly work. Ps114

Turn my land of lack in to a valley of abundance. Ps114

In the name of the Lord Jesus Christ I pray.

Prayer Set 150

Holy Father, empower my heart to love others as you love me. 2Tim11

Let whatever I say reflect your love and your kindness. 2Tim12

Teach me to talk positively about people and to see greatness in their lives, and help me avoid slandering their weaknesses. 2Tim13

Give me the grace and favor to explore the riches and territories you set for me to conquer. Ps115

Bless the gift and my portion you set for me so I can enjoy your prosperity peacefully and without sorrow for your glory. Ps115

Let your loving-kindness and your goodness motivate my soul to please you always. Ps115

Anoint me to firmly rely on you because of your unfailing love and trustworthiness. Ps115

Receive my praise favorably. Ps115

In the name of the Lord Jesus Christ I pray.

Prayer Set 151

Holy Father, empower me to use my financial wealth as a servant to magnify your holy will in my hand but not as an idol to worship. 8

Give me the grace to remain for all my life in the instructions of your holy Word through the Lord Jesus Christ and your holy apostles. 1Tim9

Give me contentment in your joyful presence in me. 1Tim10

Empower me to remain humble while having great wealth and to put my hope only in you rather than riches. 1Tim11

Thank you for all my prayers you have answered. Ps116

Empower my soul to always show gratitude to you through prayers of thanksgiving and songs of praise in good and bad times alike. Ps116

Thank you for your blessed and joyful presence in me that takes away all my distress and anxiety. Ps116

Thank you for your help and instructions that make me wiser every day so I can live holy in your presence. Ps116

In the name of the Lord Jesus Christ I pray.

Prayer Set 152

Holy Father, rekindle in my heart and mind the ability to prioritize in my life sanctification, purity of heart and mind, and holy living through all my conduct. 1Thes7

Teach me to learn wisely, prudently, and with deep insight your holy Word and to take seriously the instruction from the Lord Jesus Christ and his apostles. 1Thes8

Give me a diligent hand and the wisdom to manage excellently the work and the business you entrust to me. 1Thes9

Teach me to be respectful of all those who are serving you in the ministry, to be discreet about their personal weaknesses, and to gracefully and lovingly pray for them. 1Thes10

Give me a loving heart to encourage immature Christians and support them with patience. 1Thes12

Empower me to bring multitudes to worship you in spirit and truth. Ps117

Let my life be a perfect example of holy living so others will have the fear and love of you. Ps117

In the name of the Lord Jesus Christ I pray.

Prayer Set 153

Holy Father, thank you for the gift of salvation and your forgiveness of my sin through the blood of the Lord Jesus Christ. Ps118

Empower me to develop the habit of praising you every day. Ps118

Give me a strong awareness of your comforting presence all the time but more so in times of distress. Ps118

Remind me to call on you for help when I do not find answers for my unbearable problems and when I am failing spiritually. Ps118

Teach me to always overcome the traps of my enemies. Ps118

Let me always rely in you for everything, and embolden my faith in you. Ps118

Cut the cords of the wicked and the chains of the power of darkness on my soul and life. Ps118

Burn to ashes every evil spirit that comes to trample my health and spiritual life. Ps118

Pour a prosperous blessing on me from the gates of heaven. Ps118

Give me the gift to exalt you with songs of praise and thanksgiving at home and in great assemblies. Ps118

In the name of the Lord Jesus Christ I pray.

Prayer Set 154

Holy Father, provide me a strong desire to submit myself totally to you. Ps119

Let my soul be an embodiment of praise to you in humility of heart and in holy living. Ps119

Give me a heart that longs for your Word and has greater insight into it. Ps119

Strengthen and motivate me to live according to your instructions. Ps119

Enlighten my heart and spirit to take immense joy and comfort to practice your holy Word. Ps119

Let me always deeply understand your holy Word to better apply it to my life. Ps119

Give me the wisdom to admire the goodness of your words that you give me to obey. Ps119

Isolate my eyes and soul from evilness and everything that does not bring glory to you. Ps119

Materialize in my life everything that you pledge to give me so I can help others repent and live holy lives. Ps119

Increase my expectation in you, and let your holy Word be always in my mind. Ps119

In the name of the Lord Jesus Christ I pray.

Prayer Set 155

Holy Father, give me the devotion to present my body to you as a holy vessel in upright living. Ro4

Give me the grace to master, dominate, and overcome sin with great authority. Ro5

Motivate me to obey your Word and to become a slave of righteousness. Ro6

Wipe away the plans and traps of the power of darkness to destroy and plunder me. Ps120

Motivate and empower me to take authority by using your spiritual weapons to defeat the kingdom of darkness. Ps120

Cast away the presence of evil spirits from my soul and house. Ps120

Vanquish the power that blocks my sovereign right to prosper. Ps120

In the name of the Lord Jesus Christ I pray.

Prayer Set 156

Holy Father, remind me that you are willing to always help me get out of a sinful life if I am willing to call on you for help and to find spiritual help in my church. Ro1

Give me the courage to look for help when I am ensnared in sin. Ro2

Train me to trample sin under my feet and boldly reject all wicked desires and thoughts. Ro3

Bless me abundantly to humble the arrogant who believe in their rich prosperity. Ps72

Give me the grace to use your eye salve to help arrogant people see and become humble so they can regard everyone as significant as they are. Ps72

Manifest your wisdom in me to reach the heart of arrogant individuals so they can come to repentance and salvation. Ps72

Prosper me in wisdom, godliness, and financial wealth to attract the prideful to humility. Ps72

Predispose my heart to forgive everyone in advance and to be compassionate for people who are arrogant and offensive and want to trample my and others' souls. Ps72

In the name of the Lord Jesus Christ I pray.

Part 14

For He satisfies the longing soul, and fills the hungry soul with goodness. (Psalm 107:9 NKJV)

Prayer Set 157

Holy Father, protect your holy students from the immoral and atheistic indoctrination of the secular school system that teaches contrary to Holy Scripture. Ps74

Let your holy Word prevail over the realm of darkness and corruption of this world and mostly in my country. Ps74

Empower Christian parents to protect their children from the spiritual darkness in this world, which gets its strength from the social media and the ungodly educational system in our society. Ps74

Do not let us be blind and perish under the domination of this world system of entertainment that does not reflect your holy Word. Ps74

Allow a successful, global spiritual revival movement for your holy people who have been spiritually asleep due to the social confusion of the world culture that predominates now. Ps74

Rain the river that rejoices your city in heaven on all people to bring them to repentance and salvation. Ps74

Deliver us from the bondage of the power of darkness in this world just as you brought the Israelites out of Egypt. Ps74

In the name of the Lord Jesus Christ I pray.

Prayer Set 158

Holy Father, strengthen and empower me to joyfully obey your holy Word with the guidance of the Holy Spirit. Pet1

Rekindle your holy anointing of devotion on me to magnify a passionate desire in my heart to show holiness with all my conduct. Pet2

Magnify your love in my soul so I can joyfully offer you my body as a living sacrifice in godliness and to walk before you with integrity. Pet3

Remind me often that I am with your special people, a holy nation, a royal priesthood, and your choicest portion. Pet4

Give me a loving heart to pray for the salvation of unsaved people who live in abundant prosperity and who are in powerful governmental positions. Ps75

Pour on my soul the spirit of compassion and wisdom to devote my prayers on behalf of multitudes in a way to successfully bring them to full repentance and your salvation. Ps75

Remind me about the judgment on the ungodly and the provision of justice to salvage humankind. Ps75

Empower me always to bring praise to you. Ps75

In the name of the Lord Jesus Christ I pray.

Prayer Set 159

Holy Father, overflow my soul daily with your love for everyone.

Empower me to meditate often on how to help people in need of food, money, and shelter. 1Jo13

Show me how to practice your love toward everyone. 1Jo14

Teach me better how to pray to you perfectly and according to your will. 1Jo15

Give me the grace to dispel the glory of your holy name to the ends of the earth. Ps76

Empower me with the courage to sincerely renew my commitment to obey and follow you perfectly with all my heart. Ps76

Train me to proclaim your eternal sovereignty as above all powers and every creation and to persuade multitudes to come to your salvation. Ps76

In the name of the Lord Jesus Christ I pray.

Prayer Set 160

Holy Father, speak to me when I call you in times of trouble. Manifest your comfort and strength in me when my soul is sorrowful. Ps77

Provide me the faith and the insurance that all my prayers will be answered, and give me the patience to wait for your answers. Ps77

Enlighten my heart so I can meditate on the truthfulness in your holy Word and on your gracefulness toward all your holy children. Ps77

Manifest your joy, love, and peace in my soul, and let my hope in you be like a river that overflows in my heart every day. Ps77

Show me, Lord, that your compassion will never end for me when I am in times of crisis. Ps77

Inspire me and teach me more about your compassionate intervention and work of redemption to redeem the world to salvation. Ps77

Give me the strength and wisdom to exalt you all the time. Ps77

Open the stores of heaven, and pour day and night all kinds of blessing on my life to exhibit your abundant wealth on earth for your glory. De48

In the name of the lord Jesus Christ I pray.

Prayer Set 161

Holy Father, increase your fear and love in me when frustration from this life saddens my heart. Ps78

Train me to always respond with gentleness and kindness to those who verbally abuse me. Ps78

Give me the conscience to never take for granted your grace of salvation and your daily blessings. Ps78

Show me how to avoid everything that could lead me to sin. Ps78

Teach me and empower me to live a sinless life. Ps78

Inspire me daily to show gratitude to you for your love and all the goodness you have freely given to me. Ps78

Strengthen me to walk faithfully with you in sincerity of heart. Ps78

Motivate me to prioritize your holy precepts in my life above everything. Ps78

Teach me to be always in your presence. Ps78

Preserve me from the deceit and traps of the kingdom of darkness. Ps78

Establish me in prosperity in my land in unity with you and in godliness to praise and honor you. Ps78

In the name of the Lord Jesus Christ I pray.

Prayer Set 162

Holy Father, pour a mighty rain of spiritual revival on the earth and my house so my family and I can be a productive part of this glorious event. Ps79

Convince my heart daily to boldly follow all your precepts in full obedience to your holy Word by the power of your grace. Ps78

Create in me a heart that is passionate to please and honor you with all my possessions. Ps79

Let me clearly acknowledge your eternal sovereignty over your creation to bring fear of you to the ungodly. Ps79

Let all nations be aware of your sovereignty so they can abide by the principles of your holy kingdom. Ps79

Deliver me and my nation spiritually from the wickedness of this world by the blood of the Lamb. Ps79

In the name of the Lord Jesus Christ I pray.

Prayer Set 163

Holy Father, let me become not a vase of mockery among your holy people but instead an honorable vase. Ps80

Empower me to be always a vase of honor for your glory. Ps80

Let me never walk in shame. Ps80

Deliver me from the wrath of my adversaries, and let my failures bring forth wisdom in my soul to unfailingly triumph in holiness and financial prosperity over this troubled and wicked world. Ps80

Empower me to attain every blessing you have for me so my life can bring glory to you in prosperity. Ps80

Increase my expectations for your blessed promises you have proclaimed over my life. Ps80

Let your blessed promises over my life empower me to bring praise and glory to you everywhere. Ps80

In the name of the Lord Jesus Christ I pray.

Prayer Set 164

Holy Father, heal me from my weaknesses and show me the steps that drive me to iniquity and spiritual sicknesses so I can boldly avoid them for all my life. 1Jo10

Let me be fully aware of everything that poisons my soul to keep me in sin. 1Jo11

Empower me to always do what is right in your eyes. 1Jo12

Provide me a mind and heart that are submitted to you. Ps81

Anoint my heart and mind to obey all your commands and instructions. Ps81

Strength my soul to be totally devoted and submitted to you and at your service, and enlighten my eyes to see clearly the path, the vision, and the work you planned for me. Ps81

Let me not stay on my own way and disregard your commands and instructions. Ps81

In the name of the Lord Jesus Christ I pray.

Prayer Set 165

Holy Father, purify my heart and wipe away lustful desires. Help me avoid vain things of the world. 1Jo7

Empower me not to be boastful about my wealth and my achievements. Clothe me with humility, and let my light shine always. 1Jo8

Let your will prosper in my hand so I can fulfill your plan for my life. 1Jo9

Bring justice, honesty, and integrity to all private and governmental institutions in charge of justice and the banking system; motivate them to engage wholeheartedly in helping and investing productively in vulnerable citizens and countries. Ps82

Wipe away laws that support immorality everywhere, and bring new laws that conform to the Holy Scripture. Ps82

Open my eyes and understanding so I can comprehend and see the deceitful activities of the power of darkness through all cultural activities in this world that have become the normal way of living in this world. Ps82

In the name of the Lord Jesus Christ I pray.

Prayer Set 166

Holy Father, reveal to all Christians the entrapping agenda of the kingdom of darkness through every culture that bring Christians to spiritual death and blindness. Ps83

Empower me to faithfully distance myself from every ambush of the realm of darkness. Ps83

Give me the favor and power to take back every blessing the kingdom of darkness has stolen from me. Ps83

Shame all the activities of the kingdom of darkness so people can repent and be saved. Ps83

Restore to me seven times over everything the kingdom of darkness has stolen from me. Ps83

Empower me to praise you with songs and thanksgiving melodies at home and in public. Ps83

In the name of the Lord Jesus Christ I pray.

Prayer Set 167

Holy Father, give me a permanent anointing to long for you every day to seek more of your comforting, loving, and joyful presence. Ps84

Empower me to seek and to long for your holiness more. Ps84

Let my soul be a welcoming and pleasant recipient of the Holy Spirit. Ps84

Allow your joy to never depart from me, and cause me to always depend on your holy presence above all else. Ps84

Let your light shine through my heart and mind to manifest your holy kingdom everywhere. Ps84

Empower me to faithfully walk always in uprightness before you. Ps84

Increase my confidence every day in your unfailing love to proclaim your mercy and grace through the death and resurrection of your beloved Son Jesus Christ. Ps84

In the name of the Lord Jesus Christ I pray.

Prayer Set 168

Holy Father, let me joyfully rely on your Holy Spirit in me and manifest your joyfulness, peace, and love in my heart. Ps97

Allow me to be aware of and witness your mighty blessings that bring fulfillment and satisfaction to my soul. Ps97

Blaze your mighty fire of protection around me to keep the wicked spiritual powers away from me. Ps97

Cause your light to remain shining over me to bring people to repentance and salvation. Ps97

Empower me to idolize nothing worldly. Ps97

Guide me always to successfully avoid the sinful traps of the enemy. Ps97

In the name of the Lord Jesus Christ I pray. Ps97

Part 15

Do not turn away from your flesh and blood. Then your light will break forth like the dawn and your healing will quickly appear. (Isaiah 58:7–8)

Prayer Set 169

Holy Father, empower me to always bring my concerns to you and to always humble myself under your mighty hand. Pet11

Increase my strength and courage to resist the devil and all his evil spirits. Pet12

Bless me with a tender heart to profoundly love everyone in a godly way. Pet13

Thank you for sending your beloved Son Jesus Christ to take our eternal judgment and for providing me the full provision to live a holy life. Ps98

Thank you for washing away my sins in the blood of my Lord Jesus Christ. Ps98

Empower me to joyfully sing songs of thanksgiving and praise to you. Ps98

Thank you for attracting me to your beloved Son, who saved my soul. Ps98

Empower me to proclaim that good news all over earth, and let the mighty justice you provide the world to reach every heart and soul and save them. Ps98

In the name of the Lord Jesus Christ I pray.

Prayer Set 170

Holy Father, give me the grace to courageously persevere in obedience to you when the cross of my sinful flesh, of my personal weaknesses, and of the tribulations in this life are distressfully burdening my soul. Heb8

Empower me with biblical knowledge to never fall short of your grace. Heb9

Anoint me to imitate your holiness, and strengthen me to take authority over everything you give me. Ps99

Give me the power to practice lovingly and well what is right, just, and praiseworthy. Ps99

Empower my heart to passionately practice all your virtues. Ps99

Guide me to do the godly work you have called me to accomplish. Ps99

Give me a heart to love everyone impartially. Ps99

Let my praise to you be always on my lips and in my heart. Ps99

In the name of the Lord Jesus Christ I pray.

Prayer Set 171

Holy Father, empower me to be in submission to your salvation of grace that helps me avoid the ungodly ways of this world. Ti3

Give me the grace to submit to governmental authorities and pray for our leaders. Ti4

Increase a bold devotion in me to continue do what is good.

Train me to be holy in all my conduct and to live in peace with everybody. Heb10

Increase your fear and love in my heart so I can take more seriously your warnings about the devil's spiritual entrapments in this world. Heb11

Thank you for creating me to be yours and a member of your closest family. Ps100

Thank you for your loving-kindness through the salvation you provide in the Lord Jesus Christ. Ps100

Let my soul joyfully exalt you with words of thanksgiving because of your awesome goodness. Ps100

In the name of the Lord Jesus Christ I pray.

Prayer Set 172

Holy Father, give me the power, grace, and wisdom to make upright decisions every day. Ps101

Anoint my heart and mind to strongly detest the desire to sin, and empower me to never tolerate any practice of wickedness. Ps101

Empower me to lead my family and my business in godliness and integrity. Ps101

Give me the wisdom to never take pleasure in anything that does not give glory to you. Ps101

Empower and inspire the leaders of this world to bring to justice the robbers and abusers of vulnerable people. Ps101

Motivate me to successfully honor and respect your servants and holy people, and give me the wisdom and favor to keep excellent friendship with them. Ps101

Give me the courage to distance myself from wicked people and their environment whether they are rich, famous, powerful, or poor. Ps101

In the name of the Lord Jesus Christ I pray.

Prayer Set 173

Holy Father, let your right hand bring me out of the pit of financial poverty forever and from tribulation that brings soreness into my life. Ps102

Open the stores of heaven and pour day and night all kinds of blessings on my life so I can exhibit your abundant wealth on earth for your glory as it is in heaven. De48

Pour fear of you on the world and especially on lukewarm Christians. Ps102

Bring my time of your mighty favor nearer, and empower me with a bold expectation of your blessing to abide in my soul every day. Ps102

Let my eyes see your appointed time of my deliverance for unusually abundant prosperity in my live. Ps102

Manifest your blessed promises over me from your holy throne to bring people everywhere to your salvation. Ps102

Empower my loved ones to live in a godly and wise manner so they can fulfilled the blessed destiny you have planned for them. Ps102

In the name of the Lord Jesus I pray.

Prayer Set 174

Holy Father, remind me every day about the reward for those who devote their lives to please you in the Lord Jesus Christ. Ps103

Let your fear and love remain strong in mind and heart so I can please you always. Ps103

Let me abide by the ruling and cultural characteristics of your holy kingdom, and reveal to me all of them clearly through the Holy Scripture. Ps103

Cause all governmental leaders to fully support all vulnerable citizens. Ps103

Empower me and my posterity to prioritize prayer so we can live obediently and walk faithfully with your unfailing power. Ps103

Anoint me with a bold devotion for a life of praise to you in holiness and sanctification. Ps103

In the name of the Lord Jesus Christ I pray.

Prayer Set 175

Holy Father, give me the strength and grace to repent of my sin and overcome my wrongdoings that seem impossible for me to manage. Ps51

Anoint me with the favor to humbly receive the grace offered by the Lord Jesus Christ that forgives my sins so I can obey him for the rest of my life. Ps51

Let the presence of the Holy Spirit in me satisfy my soul with profound happiness every day. Ps104

Manifest the river that makes glad your holy kingdom in my life from the Holy Spirit, and let it overflow my soul. Ps104

Anoint me with the power of innovative productivity and creativity for your work and for financial productivity. Ps104

Bless me to proclaim your praise and salvation to the ends of the earth. Ps104

Let the Holy Spirit immensely magnify the power of creativity, innovation, and productivity in my live for great financial abundance and to bring more people to salvation. Ps104

In the name of the Lord Jesus Christ I pray.

Prayer Set 176

Holy Father, give me a longing heart to seek you continually in prayer and in reading the Holy Scripture every day for strength and guidance. Ps105

Bless me, and teach me to spend quality time with you every day. Ps105

Empower me to never be trampled by my foes. Ps105

Allow my life to be mightily productive in righteous works. Ps105

Empower me with your wisdom to have the financial wealth that you set for me to bring mighty productivity in godly work and to support vulnerable people. Ps105

Trouble the realm of darkness that persecutes me and steals many of my blessings; restore with your mighty hand seven times everything that was stolen from me. Ps105

Protect and deliver me and my country from economic destruction due to the harmful agenda of the kingdom of darkness through its secret, immoral, and corrupted institutions. Ps105

Open the window of heaven, and pour spiritual revival like a mighty river on my country and every other country to bring people to salvation and the church and live holy lives. Ps105

In the name of the Lord Jesus Christ I pray.

Prayer Set 177

Thank you, Lord Jesus, for bearing all my sins on the cross with extreme suffering, humiliation, and shame. Pet8

Holy Father, increase in me the power of self-control to keep my tongue and the tone of my voice holy to build up others and not harm them. Pet9

Remind me and empower me to always seek peace. Pet10

Remind me often of the great miracles and deliverances you have done in my life so I could present them to you again in thanksgiving prayers. Ps106

Motivate me not to take for granted your merciful kindness and grace. Ps106

Empower me to always put you above everything in life. Ps106

Give me the wisdom and courage to reject the sinful practices of this world that are accepted as moral and normal. Ps106

Give me the wisdom and prudence to not be ensnared by my enemy and the sinful practices of this world. Ps106

In the name of the Lord Jesus Christ I pray.

Prayer Set 178

Holy Father, give me the wisdom and the passion to proclaim your loving salvation and the awesome miracles you have done for me, my ancestors, and others. Ps107

Motivate me to always call on you and be always prudent when the enemy tries to entrap my soul in wickedness. Ps107

Show me your plan, and teach me to prioritize all your instructions. Ps107

Anoint my heart to always long for you and praise you through prayers of thanksgiving. Ps107

Draw me near to your door of blessings and deliverances so I can rejoice in you and in your holy presence without distress. Ps107

Pour your holy river into my soul to empower me to be godly and financially productive. Ps107

Empower me to nullify the spirit of curses at work to destroy and impoverish my life. Ps107

Teach me to wisely praise you in great assemblies and among powerful and famous individuals. Ps107

Give me the favor and grace to plant my financial seed in good and productive soil to reap abundant financial harvests. Ps107

Give me the power to wisely help impoverished people and fatherless hungry children. Ps107

In the name of the Lord Jesus Christ I pray.

Prayer Set 179

Holy Father, give me your fear, strength, wisdom, and knowledge to never fall away from the grace of salvation in the Lord Jesus Christ. Heb3

Increase my strength and commitment to remain obedient to you. Heb5

Let my salvation be boldly secure in your hand. Heb7

Pronounce verbally the dates of my mighty financial harvest and the success of my destiny from your holy throne, and seal it with your signet ring. Ps108

Empower me, and give me the grace to not allow the kingdom of darkness to steal my financial harvest and my destiny. Ps108

Give me the grace to successfully take authority against the kingdom of darkness. Ps108

Inspire me with new songs of praise and thanksgiving regarding your unfailing love and your unequaled power. Ps108

In the name of the Lord Jesus Christ I pray.

Prayer Set 180

Holy Father, let a strong hope in you remain in my heart when deliverance has not yet come. Ps85

Increase my trust in you when the vision you put in my spirit takes time to be accomplished. Ps85

Remind me always of your faithfulness, and empower me to please you and to boldly expect everything I have requested from you in prayer. Ps85

Teach me about all the benefits you reserve for your servants and children who live in full obedience to you. Ps85

Thank you for your salvation that you make available to all and personally to me. Ps85

Deliver me from all my enemies, and bless me with financial prosperity so I can demonstrate your merciful kindness to the ends of the world. Ps85

Let me always be content in waiting on your blessed promises. Ps85

In the name of the Lord Jesus Christ I pray.

Part 16

The Lord your God will bless you in the land he is giving you. (Deuteronomy 28:8)

Prayer Set 181

Holy Father, let the river from your holy throne water my soul, land, country, and its people with a spiritual revival and for holiness through salvation in the Lord Jesus Christ. Ps87

Manifest your glory from your holy mountain in my life so I can bring your praise and salvation to the ends of the earth. Ps87

Secure the blessed destiny you have set aside for me in the Lord Jesus by the power of your right hand so no one can plunder it. Ps87

Give me your grace and power to overcome weakness in my life so my name can be forever written in the Book of Life. Ps87

Allow that my place of residence is holy and sanctified so I can dispel your praise all the time. Ps87

Let my body be a recipient of praise in sprit and deed. Ps87

Anoint my soul to bring you sincere praise and honor. Ps87

In the name of the Lord Jesus Christ I pray.

Prayer Set 182

Holy Father, give me the wisdom to always honor my spousal relationship in a way that greatly pleases you. Heb14

Give me the spiritual wisdom and skill to manage my money well as a good servant for your glory. Heb15

Give me faithful insight that you hear my prayers favorably. 1Jo16

Teach me clearly through your Holy Scripture about the sin that leads to death. 1Jo17

Manifest your favor to me to bring your fear strongly everywhere so the wicked can come to repentance. Ps86

Empower me to be humble so I can learn from your holy people. Ps86

Deliver me from all curses that destroy my life and resources. Ps86

Teach me better how to rejoice in you continually and to better rely on your joyfulness in me. Ps86

Anoint me to praise you in sincerity of heart. Ps86

In the name of the Lord Jesus Christ I pray.

Prayer Set 183

Holy Father, let your glory be manifested in my life when the darkness and confusion in this world surround me. Ps88

Give me the courage to joyfully do awesome thing for you when troubles of many kinds assail me. Ps88

Remind me to rejoice in your presence through praise and prayer when nothing seems to work in my life. Ps88

Empower me to endure patiently and successfully the adversities of life and wrath of my foes. Ps88

Enlighten my soul in your presence to encourage me that everything will be well as I continue putting my trust in you to live faithfully. Ps88

Take me out of the financial and spiritual hole in the realm of darkness, and never allow me to be ensnared again so I can bring praise and thanksgiving to you among your people. Ps88

In the name of the Lord Jesus Christ I pray.

Prayer Set 184

Holy Father, bless and empower me to remain on your holy rock above all my enemies so I can bring fear of you to your people. Ps89

Give me your grace to pray every day for global spiritual revival. Ps89

Let your salvation break the chain of darkness to deliver vulnerable citizens from this world, and let justice flow on them like a mighty river. Ps89

Let your love and faithful compassion never depart from me and my posterity. Ps89

Make an easy way to bring me back to live a holy life when I am entrapped by my sinful weaknesses, and do not hand me over to the wrath of my enemies when you discipline me. Ps89

Cause me to be stronger in you every day and to better expect from you through thanksgiving and praise. Ps89

Strengthen me to obey your command and remain on your righteous path. Ps89

Anoint me to bring praise to you, and empower me with wisdom to magnify your glory. Ps89

In the name of the Lord Jesus Christ I pray.

Prayer Set 185

Holy Father, provide strength and excellent health for me in my old days so I can continue to proclaim your loving-kindness and salvation. Ps90

Cause my final days to not be in isolation, surround me with my loved ones and in the company of holy peoples who support me in sincerity of heart. Ps90

Let the glory of your presence shine on my face and health. Ps90

Cause me to stay close in your holy presence and to be fully aware of it every day. Ps90

Wipe away my tears, and satisfy my soul with your holy presence in me. Ps90

Manifest your holiness and your wonder exceedingly to me and my posterity. Ps90

Build me up to manifest your uprightness and salvation. Ps90

Let the prosperity of your holy kingdom fill my storehouse to declare your glory and support your holy work everywhere. Ps90

In the name of the Lord Jesus Christ I pray.

Prayer Set 186

Holy Father, train me to worship you with reverence and respect because you are glorious, highly esteemed, honorable, and loving. Heb12

Give me the power to trample every thought and image of sexual immorality that comes to my mind, and strengthen me to chastise filthiness in the name of my Lord Jesus Christ. Heb13

Show me how to abide under your mighty hand forever. Ps91

Empower me to be always submissive to your holy Word under the guidance of your right hand. Ps91

Cause my love for and hope in you to increase daily. Ps91

Let me always praise you and proclaim you as my refuge and strength; let me always seek security under your shadow. Cover me with your mighty wings when the enemy is sending its destructive weapons. Ps91

Teach me to make my soul a pleasurable environment for you and to worship you. Ps91

In the name of the Lord Jesus Christ I pray.

Prayer Set 187

Holy Father, remind me that your loving presence empowers me to be fully content. Heb16

Remind me also to share my resources with the poor. Heb17

Bless my lips to always praise you. Heb18

Let me take seriously the prophecy of the Holy Scripture. 2Pet3

Give me the grace, favor, and bold conviction to never go back to corrupt and worldly ways of living. 2Pet4

Empower me to boldly grow to maturity in the grace and knowledge of my Lord Jesus Christ. 2Pet5

Motivate me to always be on guard for biblical error incompatible with your holy Word to insure my salvation in the Lord Jesus Christ. 2Pet6

Anoint me to walk faithfully in your eyes and to please you all my life. Ps92

In the name of the Lord Jesus Christ I pray.

Prayer Set 188

Holy Father, motivate me to joyfully be a slave of righteousness forever. Pet5

Train me to sincerely love my fellow believers and be courteous to everyone. Pet6

Give me the wisdom to properly honor government officials and your holy servants who serve you in their ministries. Pet7

Clothe my soul with your garments of splendor and the power of the Holy Spirit. Ps93

Establish me on your solid rock so I can be unmovable when the torrent of adversities comes against me. Ps92

Fill me with joy and peace that come from the fountain of the Holy Spirit. Ps93

Let your praise be forever from my lips. Ps93

In the name of the Lord Jesus Christ I pray.

Prayer Set 189

Holy Father, deliver our nation and its citizens from those who are working to bring them down. Ps94

Wipe away the wicked plan, agenda, and laws of the kingdom of darkness by which they are trying to destroy and bring shame to my country morally and financially. Ps94

Deliver me and my posterity from violence, spiritual confusion, social immorality, and indecency. Ps94

Protect my finances, and give me awesome solutions to multiply my financial resources so I can avoid unnecessary distress. Ps94

Empower me with patience to wait and know the time of my deliverance. Ps94

Pour your love and tenderness on my soul and my posterity.

Manifest your mercy and blessings on me and my posterity to praise you. Ps94

In the name of the Lord Jesus Christ I pray.

Prayer Set 190

Holy Father, teach me your holy Word and how to meditate on it so I can successfully put it into practice. 1Jo4

Give me a bold courage to isolate myself from the things of this world that empower me to crave sinful activities. 1Jo5

Increase a bold hatred in me for any ungodly thing. 1Jo6

Give me the grace, power, and favor to practice faith, virtue, godly knowledge, self-control, patience, godliness, brotherly love, and charity as it is in your holy kingdom. 2Pet1

Empower me to humble myself so I can live in total submission to you. 2Pet2

Reveal clearly to me and to my loved ones your path, and let us always find refuge in you. Ps95

Give us a tender and a humble heart toward you, and give us a strong desire to love and obey you from generation to generation. Ps95

Let my way of living be an expression of praise and worship to you for all my life. Ps95

In the name of the Lord Jesus Christ I pray.

Prayer Set 191

Holy Father, guide me and anoint me to joyfully walk in your light daily. 1Jo

Teach me to not deviate from your light in this world. 1Jo2

Strengthen me with your fear, love, and joy to overcome sin and weaknesses. 1Jo3

Empower me to declare your glory wisely. Ps96

Anoint me with the gift of praise to worship you in spirit and truth. Ps96

Let your love and fear abide in my heart always. Ps96

Thank you for the forgiveness you freely provide me through the death and resurrection of the Lord Jesus Christ. Ps96

Thank you for writing my name in the Book of Life and for delivering me from the eternal lake of sulfuric fire. Ps96

In the name of the Lord Jesus Christ I pray.

Prayer Set 192

Holy Father, teach me to be blessed in the country I reside in permanently. De44

Show me how to always make my blessings overflow in my storehouse. De45

Provide me with the resources and wisdom to produce mighty financial harvests for your glory. De46

Establish me and my posterity as your holy people by your grace and mighty favor in your beloved son Jesus Christ. De47

Open the storehouses of heavens and pour day and night all kind of blessing on my life to exhibit your abundant wealth on earth for your glory. De48

Empower me to always remain faithful to your Word, instructions, and commands. De49

Give me the grace and favor to always be on top of my business so I can testify to your goodness to me. De50

Permit my soul to reflect who you are in my life through boundless prosperity to show the world your glory. De51

In the name of the Lord Jesus Christ I pray.

REFERENCES

Psalms

All Ps with numbers represent a psalm; for example, Ps1 represents Psalm 1.

Other References

These references are chapter references. For example, Genesis 4 means Genesis chapter 4. Those prayers were formed according to the inspiration from the chapter.

Readers will become more knowledgeable of the context of the prayer when they read the chapters in the Bible. When their prayers are brought to the Almighty, they will be more efficient because their faith will be bolder as they will have greater insight into the Word of God.

Genesis
G1 Genesis 4
G2 Genesis 1
G3 Genesis 4
G4 Genesis 6
G5 Genesis 6
G6 Genesis 12
G7 Genesis 15
G8 Genesis 22

Exodus
Ex1 Exodus 20
Ex2 Exodus 28
Ex3 Exodus 30
Ex4 Exodus 34
Ex5 Exodus 40
Ex6 Exodus 40

Leviticus
Le1 Leviticus 19; 21
Le2 Leviticus 18; 20
Le3 Leviticus 1:3–5
Le4 Leviticus
Le5 Leviticus 26
Le6 Leviticus 26
Le7 Leviticus 27

Deuteronomy
De1 Deuteronomy 32
De2 Deuteronomy 32
De3 Deuteronomy 32
De4 Deuteronomy 32
De5 Deuteronomy 32
De6 Deuteronomy 32
De7 Deuteronomy 32
De8 Deuteronomy 4
De9 Deuteronomy 10
De10 Deuteronomy 13
De11 Deuteronomy 22
De12 Deuteronomy 26
De13 Deuteronomy 27
De14 Deuteronomy 27
De15 Deuteronomy 28
De16 Deuteronomy 28
De17 Deuteronomy 28
De18 Deuteronomy 28
De19 Deuteronomy 28
De20 Deuteronomy 28
De21 Deuteronomy 28
De22 Deuteronomy 29
De23 Deuteronomy 30
De24 Deuteronomy 33
De25 Deuteronomy 33
De26 Deuteronomy 33
De27 Deuteronomy 33
De28 Deuteronomy 33
De29 Deuteronomy 33
De30 Deuteronomy 33
De31 Deuteronomy 33
De32 Deuteronomy 33
De33 Deuteronomy 33
De35 Deuteronomy 33
De36 Deuteronomy 33
De37 Deuteronomy 33
De38 Deuteronomy 33
De39 Deuteronomy 33
De40 Deuteronomy 33
De41 Deuteronomy 33
De42 Deuteronomy 33
De43 Deuteronomy 33
De44 Deuteronomy 28
De45 Deuteronomy 28
De46 Deuteronomy 28
De47 Deuteronomy 28
De48 Deuteronomy 28
De49 Deuteronomy 28
De50 Deuteronomy 28
De51 Deuteronomy 28
De52 Deuteronomy 19

Joshua and Judge
Jo1 Joshua 1
Jo2 Joshua 1
Jo3 Joshua 1
Jo4 Joshua 1
Jo5 Joshua 1
Jo6 Joshua 1
Jo7 Joshua 1
Jo8 Joshua 1
Jo9 Joshua 7
Jo10 Joshua 10
Jo11 Joshua 19

Jo12 Joshua 24
Ju1 Judge 5
Ju2 Judge 5
Ju3 Judge 6

1Samuel
1Sa1 Samuel 3
1Sa2 Samuel 3
1Sa3 Samuel 12
1Sa4 Samuel 12
1Sa5 Samuel 12

2 Samuel, Ezra and Nehemiah
2 Sa1 2 Samuel
2 Sa2 2 Samuel 5
2 Sa3 2 Samuel 10
2 Sa4 2 Samuel 12
2 Sa5 2 Samuel 22
2Sa6 2 Samuel 22
2Sa7 2 Samuel 22
2Sa8 2 Samuel 22
2Sa9 2 Samuel 22
2Sa10 2 Samuel 22
2Sa11 2 Samuel 22
2Sa12 2 Samuel 22
2Sa13 2 Samuel 22
2Sa14 2 Samuel
2Sa15 2 Samuel
2Sa16 2 Samuel 22
2Sa17 2 Samuel 22
2Sa19 2 Samuel 22
2Sa20 2 Samuel 28
2Sa21 2 Samuel 24
2Sa22 2 Samuel
Ez23 Ezra 10
Ne24 Nehemiah 3
Ne25 Nehemiah 6
Ne26 Nehemiah 5
Ne27 Nehemiah 8
Ne28 Nehemiah 9

Proverbs
Pr1 Proverbs 1
Pr2 Proverbs 1
Pr3 Proverbs 1
Pr4 Proverbs 1
Pr5 Proverbs 1
Pr6 Proverbs 1
Pr7 Proverbs 2
Pr8 Proverbs 2
Pr9 Proverbs 2
Pr10 Proverbs 3
Pr11 Proverbs 3
Pr12 Proverbs 3
Pr13 Proverbs 3
Pr14 Proverbs 3
Pr15 Proverbs 3
Pr16 Proverbs 4
Pr16b Proverbs 4
Pr17 Proverbs 29:5–7
Pr18 Proverbs 22: 5–7
Pr19 Proverbs 5
Pr20 Proverbs 5
Pr21 Proverbs 6:7
Pr23 Proverbs 9
Pr24 Proverbs 9
Pr25 Proverbs 10
Pr26 Proverbs 10
Pr27 Proverbs 11
Pr28 Proverbs 11
Pr29 Proverbs 11
Pr30 Proverbs 13
Pr31 Proverbs 15
Pr32 Proverbs 15

Pr33 Proverbs 16
Pr34 Proverbs 19
Pr35 Proverbs 19
Pr36 Proverbs 22
Pr37 Proverbs 22
Pr38 Proverbs 22
Pr39 Proverbs 23
Pr40 Proverbs 23
Pr41 Proverbs 28
Pr42 Proverbs 28
Pr43 Proverbs 28
Pr44 Proverbs 29
Pr45 Proverbs 29
Pr46 Proverbs 31
Pr47 Proverbs 31

Ecclesiastes
Ec1 Ecclesiastes 7
Ec2 Ecclesiastes 7
Ec3 Ecclesiastes 7

Isaiah
Is1 Isaiah 53
Is2 Isaiah 57
Is3 Isaiah 58
Is4 Isaiah
Is5 Isaiah 32
Is6 Isaiah 32
Is7 Isaiah 35
Is8 Isaiah 44
Is9 Isaiah 44
Is10 Isaiah 44
Is11 Isaiah 50
Is12 Isaiah 49
Is13 Isaiah 51

Jeremiah
Je1 Jeremiah 30
Je2 Jeremiah 30
Je3 Jeremiah 30
Je4 Jeremiah 30
Je5 Jeremiah 30
Je6 Jeremiah 31
Je7 Jeremiah 31
Je8 Jeremiah 31
Je9 Jeremiah 33
Je10 Jeremiah 33
Je11 Jeremiah 33
Je12 Jeremiah 33

Malachi
Mal 1 Malachi 2
Mal 2 Malachi 2
Mal 4 Malachi 3

Matthew
Ma1 Matthew 4
Ma2 Matthew 4
Ma3 Matthew 4
Ma4 Matthew 4
Ma5 Matthew 4
Ma6 Matthew 4
Ma7 Matthew 4
Ma8 Matthew 4
Ma9 Matthew 4
Ma10 Matthew 5
Ma11 Matthew 5
Ma12 Matthew 5
Ma13 Matthew 5
Ma14 Matthew 5
Ma15 Matthew 5
Ma16 Matthew 5
Ma17 Matthew 6

Ma18 Matthew 6
Ma19 Matthew 6
Ma20 Matthew 6
Ma21 Matthew 6
Ma22 Matthew 6
Ma23 Matthew 7
Ma24 Matthew 7
Ma25 Matthew 7
Ma26 Matthew 7
Ma27 Matthew 7
Ma28 Matthew 7
Ma29 Matthew 7
Ma30 Matthew 9
Ma31 Matthew 10
Ma32 Matthew 10
Ma33 Matthew 10
Ma34 Matthew 10
Ma35 Matthew 13
Ma36 Matthew 13
Ma37 Matthew 13
Ma38 Matthew 13
Ma39 Matthew 16
Ma40 Matthew 18
Ma41 Matthew 18
Ma42 Matthew 19
Ma43 Matthew 23
Ma44 Matthew 28
Ma45 Matthew 28
Ma46 Matthew 28
Ma47 Matthew 28
Ma48 Matthew 28

John
Joh1 John 14
Joh2 John 17
Joh3 John 21

Acts
Ac1 Acts 2
Ac2 Acts 2
Ac3 Acts 4
Ac4 Acts 4
Ac5 Acts 4
Ac6 Acts 6
Ac7 Acts 9
Ac8 Acts 9
Ac9 Acts
Ac10 Acts 10
Ac11 Acts 20
Ac12 Acts 10
Ac13 Acts 10
Ac14 Acts 28

Romans
Ro1 Romans 6
Ro2 Romans 6
Ro3 Romans 6
Ro4 Romans 6
Ro5 Romans 6
Ro6 Romans 6
Ro7 Romans 6
Ro8 Romans 6
Ro9 Romans 6
Ro10 Romans 6
Ro11 Romans 6
Ro12 Romans 6
Ro13 Romans 7
Ro14 Romans 8
Ro15 Romans 8
Ro16 Romans 8
Ro17 Romans 8
Ro18 Romans 8
R019 Romans 12
Ro20 Romans

Ro21 Romans
Ro22 Romans 13

2 Corinthians
2Co 2Corinthians 6

Galatians
Ga1 Galatians 5
Ga2 Galatians 5
Ga3 Galatians 5
Ga4 Galatians 5
Ga5 Galatians 5
Ga6 Galatians 5
Ga7 Galatians 6
Ga8 Galatians 6

Ephesians
Ep1 Ephesians 3
Ep2 Ephesians 3
Ep3 Ephesians 4
Ep4 Ephesians 4
Ep5 Ephesians 4
EP6 Ephesians 4
Ep7 Ephesians 4
Ep8 Ephesians 4
Ep9 Ephesians 5
Ep10 Ephesians 5
Ep11 Ephesians 5
Ep12 Ephesians 5, 6
Ep13 Ephesians 6

Philippians
Ph1 Philippians 1
Ph1 Philippians 2
Ph3 Philippians 2
Ph4 Philippians 2
Ph5 Philippians 3
Ph6 Philippians 4
Ph7 Philippians 4
Ph8 Philippians 4
Ph9 Philippians 4
Ph10 Philippians 4
Ph11 Philippians 4
Ph12 Philippians 4
Ph13 Philippians 3

Colossians
Col1 Colossians 1
Col2 Colossians 1
Col3 Colossians 2
Col4 Colossians 2
Col5 Colossians 2
Col6 Colossians 2
Col7 Colossians 3
Col8 Colossians 3
Col9 Colossians 3
Col10 Colossians 3
Col11 Colossians 3
Col12 Colossians 4
Col13 Colossians 4
Col14 Colossians 4
Col15 Colossians 4
Col16 Colossians 4

1 Thessalonians
1Thes1 1Thessalonians 1
1Thes2 1Thessalonians 3
1Thes3 1Thessalonians 3
1Thes4 1Thessalonians 3
1Thes5 1Thessalonians 4
1Thes6 1Thessalonians 4
1Thes7 1Thessalonians 4
1Thes8 1Thessalonians 4

1Thes9 1Thessalonians--
1Thes10 1Thessalonians 5
1Thes 1Thessalonians 5
1Thes11 1Thessalonians 5
1Thes12 1Thessalonians 5
1Thes13 1Thessalonians 5
1Thes14 1Thessalonians 5
1Thes15 1Thessalonians 5
1Thes16 1Thessalonians 5
1Thes17 1Thessalonians 5

2 Thessalonians
2Thes18 2Thessalonians 3
2Thes19 2Thessalonians 3

1Timothy
1Tim1 1Timothy 2
1Tim2 1Timothy 2
1Tim3 1Timothy 2
1Tim4 1Timothy 2
1Tim5 1Timothy 2
1Tim6 1Timothy 2
1Tim7 1Timothy 6
1Tim8 1Timothy-
1Tim9 1Timothy 6
1Tim10 1Timothy 6
1Tim11 1Timothy 6

2 Timothy
2Tim1 2Timothy 2
2Tim2 2Timothy 2
2Tim3 2Timothy 2
2Tim4 2Timothy 2
2Tim5 2Timothy 3
2Tim6 2Timothy 3
2Tim7 2Timothy 3
2Tim8 2Timothy
2Tim9 2Timothy 3
2Tim10 2Timothy 3
2Tim11 2Timothy 3
2Tim12 2Timothy 3
2Tim13 2Timothy 3
2Tim14 2Timothy 3
2Tim15 2Timothy 3
2Tim16 2Timothy 3
2Tim17 2Timothy 4
2Tim18 2Timothy 4
2Tim19 2Timothy 4
2Tim20 2Timothy 4
2Tim21 2Timothy 4

Titus
Ti1 Titus 1
Ti2 Titus 2
Ti3 Titus 2
Ti4 Titus 3
Ti5 Titus 3

Hebrews
Heb1 Hebrews 2
Heb2 Hebrews 2
Heb3 Hebrews 6
Heb4 Hebrews 10
Heb5 Hebrews 10
Heb6 Hebrews 10
Heb7 Hebrews
Heb8 Hebrews 12
Heb9 Hebrews 12
Heb10 Hebrews 12
Heb11 Hebrews 12
Heb12 Hebrews 12
Heb13 Hebrews 13
Heb14 Hebrews 13

Heb15 Hebrews 13
Heb16 Hebrews 13
Heb17 Hebrews 13
Heb18 Hebrews 13

1 Peter
1Pet1 1Peter 1
1Pet2 1Peter 1
1Pet3 1Peter 1
1Pet4 1Peter 2
1Pet5 1Peter 2
1Pet6 1Peter 2
1Pet7 1Peter 2
1Pet8 1Peter 2
1Pet9 1Peter
1Pet10 1Peter 3
1Pet11 1Peter 5
1Pet12 1Peter 5
1Pet13 1Peter 4

2 Peter
2Pet1 2Peter 1
2Pet2 2Peter 1
2Pet3 2Peter 1
2Pet4 2Peter 2
2Pet5 2Peter 3
2Pet6 2Peter 3

1 John
1Jo1 1John 1
1Jo2 1John 1
1Jo3 1John 2
1Jo4 1John 5:2–3
1Jo5 1John 2
1Jo6 1John 2
1Jo7 1John 2
1Jo8 1John 2
1Jo9 1John 2
1Jo10 1John 3 5
1Jo11 1John 3 5
1Jo12 1John 3
1Jo13 1John 3
1Jo14 1John 4–5
1Jo15 1John 5
1Jo16 1John 5
1Jo17 1John 5

2 John
2Jo1 2John 1
2Jo3 2John 1

Revelation
Re1 Revelation 2
Re2 Revelation
Re3 Revelation 2
Re4 Revelation 2
Re5 Revelation 2
Re6 Revelation 2
Re7 Revelation 2
Re8 Revelation 2
Re9 Revelation 3
Re10 Revelation 3
Re11 Revelation 3
Re12 Revelation 3
Re13 Revelation--
Re14 Revelation 3
Re15 Revelation 3
Re16 Revelation 3
Re17 Revelation 3

CPSIA information can be obtained
at www.ICGtesting.com
Printed in the USA
FFHW021101041119
55888262-61770FF